ACTION REPLAYS

Text copyright © Steve Barlow, Iain Carter, Steve Skidmore, 1996

All rights reserved. No part of this publication may be reproduced, stored in a retrieval system, or transmitted in any form or by any means electronic, mechanical, photocopying, recording or otherwise, without the prior permission of the copyright owner.

The right of Steve Barlow, Iain Carter and Steve Skidmore to be identified as Authors of this work has been asserted by them in accordance with the Copyright, Designs and Patents Act 1988.

Designed by Paul Cooper Design

Printed and bound by Progressive Printing, Leigh-on-Sea for the publishers Piccadilly Press Ltd., 5 Castle Road, London NW1 8PR

A catalogue record for this book is available from the British Library

ISBN: 1 85340 328 8 (hardback)
1 85340 323 7 (trade paperback)

Steve Barlow is a teacher who lives in Heanor, Derbyshire. He has written several books in collaboration with Steve Skidmore, including: *Get Better Grades, Get Better Grades – Maths*, and *In Love With An Urban Gorilla*.

Iain Carter lives in Surbiton, Surrey. He is a sports broadcaster and works for Radio 5. This is his first book.

Steve Skidmore lives in Birstell, Leicestershire. He spends his time teaching, writing and watching Leicester Tigers.

ACTION REPLAYS

Steve Barlow • Iain Carter • Steve Skidmore

Piccadilly Press • London

CONTENTS

Introduction 1

ACTION REPLAYS 2-76
Sir Stanley Matthews 2
Football Fanatical: Steve Skidmore 7
Gary Lineker 10
Vinnie Jones 16
Football Fanatical: Fran Blackler 21
Robert Lee 23
Football Fanatical: Steve Barlow 27
Terry Butcher 31
Football Fanatical: Garry Richardson 36
Chris Waddle 39
Football Fanatical: Alan Green 43
Steve Bruce 47
Football Fanatical: Pete Taylor 51
Andy Townsend 53
Debbie Bampton 58
Football Fanatical: John Heath 62
Sir Bobby Charlton 64
Tony Adams 70
Football Fanatical: Iain Carter 75

THE ANORAK SECTION 77-139
Who Or What Are Anoraks? 77
Are You A Footballing Anorak? 77
Weird Facts 80
Results 83

Introduction

When we were asked to compile *Action Replays*, we were over the moon. Here was an opportunity to talk to some of the greatest players ever about their favourite footballing moments *and* help out a charity at the same time. There was everything to play for.

We decided it was going to be a book of two halves: Action Replays and a section for Anoraks that would keep budding Statos in their dressing gowns for the next ten years, or until England beat Germany, whichever is sooner.

Mind you, it was a funny old game trying to get hold of the players. In some cases, we had to talk to their agents, their answerphones, their kids, parents, pet budgies etc first. Nevertheless, we kept going to the final whistle and gave it 110 per cent. We thought some of the stories we were told showed real class, so all credit to the players. The lads done good.

When we couldn't get hold of a player, we were as sick as a parrot, but we put that one behind us and took it one player at a time. You win some, you lose some.

At the end of the day, we got the result we wanted: a book completely free of footballing clichés.

Barlow, Carter, Skidmore

ACTION REPLAYS

SIR STANLEY MATTHEWS

Action Replays Factfile

**Born
February 1st 1915
in Hanley,
Stoke-on-Trent**

ACTION REPLAYS

Action Replays Factfile

1932	Became professional with Stoke City
1934	First capped for England against Wales
1946	Bought by Blackpool for £11,500
1961	Returned to Stoke for £2,800 at the age of 46
1965	Retired at the age of 50!
1965-68	General Manager of Port Vale
1970	Manager of Hibernian (Malta)

Clubs

Stoke City (1932-46), Blackpool (1946-61)
Stoke City (1961-65)

Honours

54 caps for England (over 22 years)
Played 84 games for England (including war time internationals)
1948 English Footballer of the Year
1963 English Footballer of the Year
1956 European Footballer of the Year
1953 FA Cup Winners Medal
1957 Awarded the CBE
1965 Knighted

Action Replays

Stanley Matthews was, quite simply, one of the greatest players of football in the world – *ever*!

He had the nickname "Wizard of Dribble" and as an outside right, would beat opposition full backs with his body swerve and great acceleration.

During the 1930s and 40s he was considered the greatest right winger in the world and was loved by crowds everywhere. He was a real ambassador of the game and like Gary Lineker, never received a booking or was sent off. Not surprisingly, in a career that lasted so long and had so many memorable moments, Stanley Matthews can't pick any one particular Action Replay.

"The magic moments of my career were not provided by any particular moment on the field. Instead, it was always in the dressing room immediately before I went out to play.

"An hour before the kick off, you get stripped, you have a shower. You know very well you want to win, to play well but you don't know whether it will happen. You have butterflies and to me that was always the most exciting time.

"To be in the dressing room when there are fifty thousand spectators outside, you knew if we won you'd have a good night's sleep, if you lost you wouldn't sleep so well.

"I honestly can't pick out one game. Everyone talks about the Matthews Cup Final in 1953, but I always remember that for Stan Mortensen's hat trick."

This game took place at Wembley Stadium on May 2nd 1953 between Matthews's Blackpool and the brilliant Bolton Wanderers. It is now regarded by many as being the greatest FA Cup final ever played. Stanley Matthews was aged 38 and had already played in two Cup finals with Blackpool, only to receive a loser's medal both times.

With only 20 minutes remaining of the '53 final, Blackpool

ACTION REPLAYS

were down 3-1, and it looked as though Matthews would end up again on a losing side.

But then the two Stans took over...

Stanley Matthews set spectators jumping when his centre was cracked into the Bolton net by Stan Mortensen for his second goal of the game – 3-2!

As the clock ticked down it seemed that Matthews's dream of a Cup final medal would not happen.

However, with just one minute to go, Stan Mortensen completed his hat trick with a cracking free kick to level the score at 3-3. (He is still the only man to have scored a hat trick in an FA Cup final.) Then in the last minute, Stanley Matthews received the ball and went off on a dazzling run down the right wing. His cross was met by Bill Perry whose shot past the Bolton keeper and defenders to win the Cup for Blackpool. It become known as the Matthews Final, even though Stan Mortensen scored three times!

In an international career that lasted for 22 years, Sir Stanley also remembers the magic of playing for England.

"It was extra special playing for England; when you wore your country's shirt it made you very proud indeed. Nevertheless, all I ever wanted to do was my best and it didn't matter who I was playing for or whether it was just a friendly. I couldn't afford to let my reputation go down in any game.

"I never thought it was anything special to carry on playing until I was 50. In my time most players' careers came to an end at about 32. When I got to that age I felt fine and I kept going. You know the goal to success is enthusiasm and I had loads to carry on.

"I wanted to stay fit and I just carried on until I was 50. In fact I think I retired 2 years too early!

"I still have enthusiasm for the game. I go to watch Stoke, and it's funny, I still don't eat before a match on a Saturday. I never

did as a player and I still don't. It's nothing to do with nerves, just a habit. It's like every morning, I get up and do my exercises. I used to do it when I was 16 and still do...it's a force of habit."

SAY IT AGAIN

BYRON BUTLER

"And Wilkins sends an inch-perfect pass to no one in particular."

BUT I'M SURE HE MEANT TO...

BRIAN MOORE

"After a goalless first half, the score at half-time is 0-0."

YES, IT WOULD BE...

ACTION REPLAYS

football fanatical
Steve Skidmore

A Daisy On My Chest!

"Although I have seen many 'great' footballing moments, my Action Replay doesn't involve professional footballers.

"The moments that do involve professionals are still etched clearly in my memory (helped by watching videos of those magical moments!) and do mean something to me. For example, I can remember England winning the World Cup in 1966. I watched the match on the family's black and white telly, then spent the next six months re-living the match in the local streets and school playground with friends. No matter where we played football, the sides were always England versus West Germany. During one of these matches, I remember swearing for the first time. When I was selected for the West German team, I got 'a right 'ump on' and shouted out 'I don't want to be bl**dy West Germany!' to the amusement and 'Oooh-you-swore' consternation of my fellow six-year-old friends.

"I also have a fond memory 30 years later at Euro '96. I watched in amazement as England gave the vaunted Dutch team a 4-1 pasting (this was particularly sweet as I have several Dutch friends. Next day I sent them a fax that simply read: 'Holland 1 England 4' – I still haven't had a reply – funny that!).

"I can remember Gordon Banks's amazing save from Pele's header in the England v Brazil match during the Mexico 1970 World Cup, and also watching Manchester United and Liverpool and Aston Villa and Nottingham Forest all win the European Cup in the 70s and 80s.

"However, all of these moments were second hand; they were witnessed via the television screen – I wasn't there!

"If you are revising for an exam, it is said that the more senses

Action Replays

you use, the better you can remember things. The same applies to my Action Replay. The footballing moments that I felt, heard, touched, and even smelt and tasted are from my own school days.

"As a 10-year-old I remember playing for my school team – Highcliffe Junior School. We wore orange shirts with the school symbol on our chest. For some strange reason, the school symbol was a daisy! Not a small one, but a huge, chest-covering, white and orange monster, that wouldn't have looked out of place at the Chelsea Flower Show.

"Of course, the daisy symbol led to many opposition players letting us know what they thought of it.

"'Hello flowers.'

"'Flower power.'

"'What a team of pansies' etc etc. (This was all before political correctness, of course.)

"It also gave our loving fathers a stick with which to beat us with, when they watched us and we weren't playing well.

"'Are you sure that daisy isn't planted in the pitch – MOVE!'

"'You're playing like a limp flower – TACKLE HIM!'

"Luckily we were a half decent team so we usually managed to win games and make the opposition insults stick in their guts. Throwing the insult back at them was good as well.

"'Beaten by a load of daisies, tut, tut, you should be ashamed!'

"'Flower power rules! – you should play netball instead...' etc etc.

"But the most 'real' Action Replay for me, is a gut-wrenching wake-up-at-night-in-a-cold-sweat one.

"My home village of Birstall was (and still is) cut in two by the main A6 road. If you came from the West side of the A6 you went to the recently built Highcliffe Junior School. If you lived on the East side, you went to the older and established Riverside Junior School. The rivalry was intense between the schools (or as intense as you can get when you're 9 and 10!). Especially at sport. Especially at football.

ACTION REPLAYS

"I was playing one of my first games for the school team; and it was against Riverside – the most deadly and hated junior school rivals in the world (sorry, make that the Universe!).

"I was the number 8 – too small for defence, not skilful enough to score goals, but stupid enough to run all over the pitch!

"I remember that we were winning easily, but during the second half, for some reason unknown to me (then and now), I found myself in our own six yard box. The ball was played into my feet and in a muddle and confusion of defensive panic, I put the ball into my own goal. I can remember the horror and the sick feeling in my body as the Riverside forwards ran away laughing. All I could do was to whisper 'sorry' to my astonished looking team mates.

"Luckily we won the match 8-3, so it didn't really matter. But it did to me. It mattered a lot.

"I didn't cry though. Well, not on the pitch, not during the game. It was later that the tears came, but only when I was in the safety of my own bedroom.

"That's my Action Replay. Why? Because years later, I can still conjure up the sound, the taste, the feel, the touch and sometimes even the smell of that own goal scored in a small goal, on a small pitch by a small boy."

SAY IT AGAIN
PAT MARSDEN

"Well, gentlemen, when one team scores early in the game it often takes an early lead."

BRILLIANT!

GARY LINEKER

Action Replays Factfile

**Born
November 30th 1960
in Leicester**

ACTION REPLAYS

Clubs

Leicester City (1976-85)
Everton (1985-86)
Barcelona (Spain) (1986-89)
Tottenham Hotspur (1989-92)
Nagoya Grampus Eight (Japan) (1993-94)

Honours

1984 Appeared as sub against Scotland for his first England cap
1986 Awarded the Golden Boot for being the leading scorer in the World Cup finals
1986 PFA Footballer of the Year
1988 Spanish Cup
1989 European Cup Winners Cup
1990 FIFA Fair Play Prize
1991 FA Cup
1992 PFA Footballer of the Year
1992 Awarded the OBE

Action Replays

Lineker won 80 international caps and scored 48 times, just 1 goal away from Sir Bobby Charlton's record of 49 international goals for England.

In the whole of his playing career Lineker was never booked or sent off – a feat that was recognized by FIFA awarding him a fair play prize of £20,000 in 1990.

He is one of the greatest goalscorers England has ever had.

It is never too early for footballing glory. Goals for his local junior team, Aylestone Park in Leicester, helped pave the way for a glittering career that included the England captaincy and a Golden Boot for being the World Cup's leading scorer in 1986.

Lineker hasn't forgotten his first magic moments as a thirteen-year-old Sunday league player. As he recalled:

"There was a vital game for me for Aylestone Park. I didn't realise it at the time but the Leicester City scout was watching me. It was against a team called Wadkins. My grandad was there and he knew the City scout and asked him who he was watching, and he said the little lad up front who was quite quick. My grandad was bursting with pride after what the scout had said. Fortunately I hit the target twice and I learned about that conversation pretty quickly afterwards and there's no doubt that was the start."

He joined Leicester City and went on to win honours with Everton, Barcelona and Tottenham before heading off to Japan, where an injury eventually forced him into retirement.

Because he was such a prolific goalscorer it is difficult for Lineker to recall every goal he's ever scored.

"I don't remember every goal I scored now, although I did at

ACTION REPLAYS

one stage! I recall the important ones and certainly the England ones.

"Finishing top scorer in '86 at the World Cup finals was great and when I scored each of them it was a fantastic feeling.

"In 1990, I suppose as a one off, the feeling of exhilaration after scoring a goal was at its greatest when I scored the equaliser against West Germany in the World Cup semi-final. It was an amazing moment. People often ask me what it feels like to score such an important goal. It's impossible to describe, except to say that when you were watching that game and supporting England, you felt just like me when that goal went in – it's just 'YESSSSS!!!!' really.

"But we didn't win the game, so I wouldn't say that it was truly the magic moment of my career."

SAY IT AGAIN
DAVID COLEMAN

"On this 101st FA Cup final day, there are just two teams left."

THANK GOODNESS FOR THAT, IT WOULD HAVE GOT CROWDED ON THE PITCH IF THERE'D BEEN MORE.

Instead, Gary Lineker's Action Replay happened on May 18th 1991 at Wembley Stadium where Lineker's Tottenham Hotspurs were playing Nottingham Forest in the FA Cup final.

The game began badly for Tottenham. After just 15 minutes, Paul Gascoigne committed an awful tackle on Gary Charles just outside the Spurs box. It left Gascoigne with an injured knee and from the free kick, Stuart Pearce blasted

Action Replays

the ball through the Spurs defensive wall to put Forest in the lead.

If that wasn't a bad enough start, Lineker then had the misfortune to have a goal disallowed for offside, although the television replay showed that it clearly should have been awarded. To make matters even worse, Gary then missed a penalty after he'd been brought down by the Forest goalkeeper.

Luckily for Spurs, things got better when Paul Stewart equalised in the 55th minute and the match went into extra time.

As both sides tried to gain the upper hand, Des Walker, the Forest centre, half headed into his own goal to give Spurs a winning 2-1 scoreline.

So why was this Gary's golden moment?

"It's a bit strange because it was a game when I didn't score, I missed a penalty and I had a perfectly good goal disallowed – so maybe it's a bit of a bizarre choice. But to win the FA Cup is the dream of a lot of youngsters and I was no different. Having lost in '86 to Liverpool (for Everton), it meant so much.

"In '91 I was desperate to enjoy the experience. I haven't won too many major trophies throughout my career, so as a one off that was really special."

Lineker can recall a couple of special moments from the afternoon.

"Firstly Paul Stewart's equaliser because I did miss a penalty and if we'd lost the game I would have felt largely responsible. The relief when that goal went in, the fear was nullified and it made me feel a lot better.

"The other one was when the whistle went, not the winning goal because it was slightly tarnished as it was a Des Walker

ACTION REPLAYS

own goal and he's such a great player and a good mate. Ideally it would have been better if it had been someone else, preferably me scoring! But when that final whistle went I fell to my knees and punched the air or did something stupid like that. Climbing the steps to get my medal I wanted to be near the front. Someone had told me if you're near the back you don't really get to know what's happening.

"I saw Gary Mabbutt's face when he lifted the trophy and it's something you always want to happen and you want it to happen to yourself in many ways. But it was the next best thing for someone like Gary to do it, he epitomises all that is good in the game and it was a truly magical moment."

SAY IT AGAIN
JIMMY ARMFIELD

"John Bond has brought in a young left sided midfield player who, I guess, will play on the left side of midfield."

WELL HE WOULD, WOULDN'T HE?

LAWRIE McMENEMEY

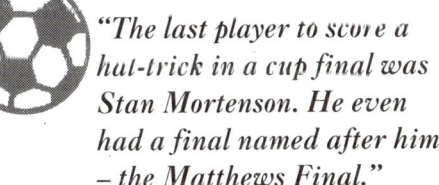

"The last player to score a hat-trick in a cup final was Stan Mortenson. He even had a final named after him – the Matthews Final."

WELL AT LEAST THEY WERE
BOTH CALLED STAN

VINNIE JONES

Action Replays Factfile

**Born
January 5th 1965
in Watford**

ACTION REPLAYS

Clubs

Wimbledon (1986-89)
Leeds United (1989-90)
Sheffield United (1990-91)
Chelsea (1991-92)
Wimbledon (1992-)

Honours

1988 FA Cup Winners Medal
1989-90 Division Two Championship
1995 Capped for Wales

Action Replays

Vinnie Jones is known as a hard man of English football: a reputation he has gained through numerous bookings and sendings off. Nevertheless, he has achieved international recognition with Wales and has won what most players dream of, an FA Cup Winners Medal.

So what is Vinnie Jones's Action Replay?

"It's very hard to know which Action Replay I would go for. It's a spin up between my Wimbledon debut and when we won the FA Cup in 1988.

"I made my debut four days after signing on at Plough Lane. It was against Manchester United and I scored the winner – what a magic moment that was."

However, Vinnie didn't impress everyone on his debut. At half time, he asked Sid, the Wimbledon kit man, how he thought his first game for Wimbledon was going. Sid replied "I'm 85 and if you gave me the number 4 shirt I'd do better!" So perhaps with Sid's words in mind, Vinnie has chosen his FA Cup triumph with Wimbledon against the mighty Liverpool in the 1988 FA Cup final at Wembley as his favourite Action Replay.

Only 11 years before their Cup final appearance, Wimbledon had been a Southern League side, but now they were in Division One. However, they faced Liverpool who had already won the League Championship and were odds on favourites to complete the double by winning the FA Cup. But Jones and his Wimbledon team mates, known affectionately (if you were a Wimbledon fan!) as the 'Crazy Gang', had other ideas.

"I suppose nothing compares with winning the Cup. No one gave us a chance against Liverpool, but the Crazy Gang always had such a great spirit, I knew we had a chance."

ACTION REPLAYS

It nearly didn't turn out quite so happily for Vinnie. In the 35th minute of the final, Liverpool's Peter Beardsley was fouled but still managed to put the ball into the Wimbledon net. However, the referee blew the whistle and awarded Liverpool a free kick instead. Whilst Liverpool were still arguing about the decision Wimbledon's Dennis Wise crossed for Laurie Sanchez who scored with a perfect header.

After that, it was never to be Liverpool's day. They missed a penalty (the first time one had ever been missed in a Wembley FA Cup final) and despite being under intense pressure, the Wimbledon defence held on to the final whistle.

SAY IT AGAIN

KEVIN KEEGAN

"I'll never play at Wembley again, unless I play there again."

OF COURSE YOU WON'T MR KEEGAN

"Laurie Sanchez scored the goal and Dave Beasant saved a penalty but what I really remember is what happened after the final whistle.

"When we'd got the cup we just wanted to charge round Wembley with it – typical crazy gang really. But the boss, Bobby Gould, just told us to slow down and make sure we enjoyed the moment with all our fans cheering us. He said it was our moment and it might never happen again."

Vinnie also has an embarrassing moment that is captured in

Action Replays

one of the most published football photos of all time.

"There've been so many embarrassing moments too...The one that stands out is when the newspapers published that picture of me marking Gazza, holding on to a part of his body that I shouldn't have been."

Which part was that? Let's just say that it bought tears to Gazza's eyes and not because he'd just been booked!

SAY IT AGAIN

MIKE CHANNON

"Believe it or not, goals can change a game."

I BELIEVE IT MICK!

MIKE ENGLAND

"Ian Rush unleashed his left foot and it hit the back of the net."

I HOPE HE GO IT BACK

MARTIN TYLER

"Oh, he had an eternity to play that ball... but he took too long over it."

DOES THIS MAN KNOW ABOUT TIME?

ACTION REPLAYS

football fanatical
Fran Blackler
Supports Nottingham Forest

"*I remember few details of matches. Before all the lads say, 'Typical female, too busy looking at footballers' legs', I'd better make it clear that the psychology which surrounds football is more interesting to me than whether a team is playing a sweeper system or not. This includes not only the game itself, or even the pre-match build-up and after match analysis; it infiltrates into every part of life. In the media, at work, with friends and strangers – football is always a friend. Everyone has an opinion on the game, even if it's 'I hate football!'*

"*Away matches, in particular, are always eventful. If there is nothing happening on the pitch there is always some off the pitch, football trivia to take back and treasure; terrible ground, good pubs, dodgy fans and another stadium ticked off to bring you closer to the elusive 91 Club. **

"*My Action Replay is Forest's away game with Chelsea in the '95-'96 season; we lost, but the company was wonderful.*

"*We met up with some exiled Leicester City fans (who, presumably for some terrible crime, had been banished from Leicester and condemned to watch football at Stamford Bridge) in the Slug and Lettuce for a pre-match drink. They were keen and optimistic, and had all the hopes in the world for their team; watching them was like seeing ourselves in a mirror. Of course, it had never occurred to our friends to change their team, even after their move to London. True fans don't (though I have a football friend who changed his allegiance from Villa simply because his gran bought him a Forest shirt one Christmas!).*

* An exclusive club you can only join by visiting all 91 away grounds in the Football League in addition to your own club's.

Action Replays

"I didn't see much of the game itself. The East Stand at Chelsea is wonderfully designed with an overhanging roof so that if you sit in one of the back five rows (which we did), you can see a letterbox-shaped bit of pitch between the roof and the rows of heads in front. Of course, when the supporters in front decided to stand up (and they seemed to feel the need to do this every other minute), we couldn't see anything at all. Being regulars at the Bridge, our Leicester friends sat in the new North Stand which has the best seats in the ground.

"After the match, happy with Forest's defeat and our misery, our Leicester friends invited us back to their flat for cups of tea, proudly served up in Leicester mugs. They showed off their newly acquired Leicester shirts and made dire threats about what the City would do to Forest once they got back in the Premiership. In that Pimlico flat, miles from home, we played out once again all the old rivalries between Filbert Street and the City Ground. We traded insults, rubbished opposition players, relived memories of players and games from years gone by...these are the good times – my most valued Action Replays.

"The bad times are those games when nothing happens, 0-0 draws where the players look lethargic, and the crowd can't get excited; where the referee doesn't make any bad decisions so you can't even get angry. And big defeats, of course. When Forest lost 5-0 to Bayern Munich in the UEFA Cup, I anticipated some jeers at work so I put up a notice saying 'No Talking About Football Today'. A colleague (who's a Tottenham supporter, sad man) took one look at the notice and hummed the German National Anthem instead!"

ROBERT LEE

Action Replays Factfile

Born
February 1st 1966
in West Ham

Action Replays

Clubs

Charlton Athletic (1983-92)
Newcastle United (1992-)

Honours

1992-3 First Division Championship
1994 England cap v Romania

ACTION REPLAYS

Rob Lee played 298 games for Charlton Athletic and scored 59 goals when Newcastle United decided that he was the striker they needed. Within a few weeks he had struck up a deadly scoring partnership with Peter Beardsley and rocketed into the footballing nation's attention. Rob realises the importance of the move north as being the big turning point of his career as it brought him to the attention of the England coach, Terry Venables.

"When I signed for Newcastle was obviously a big moment in my career. It's enabled me to go on to bigger and better things, giving me the platform to get into the England team.

"So my Action Replay would have to be making my debut for my country, when I scored against Romania at Wembley. It gave me such a thrill."

SAY IT AGAIN
JIMMY HILL

"Despite the rain, it's still raining here at Old Trafford."

STICK TO FOOTBALL, NOT
WEATHER FORECASTING, JIMMY

Rob's international debut took place at Wembley on October 12, 1994 when England took on a useful Romanian team. Things didn't quite go to plan for England and they fell behind. Then Rob took over...

"I can remember it vividly. We were one nil down at the time and things weren't going too well. Graeme Le Saux crossed the ball to the far post, to Alan Shearer. I thought, he's going to win

Action Replays

it and he nodded it straight into my path as I ran in and I put it home.

"Then Ian Wright jumped all over me and that was the last I saw of the ball. I couldn't really take it all in, it goes so quickly. One minute you're kicking off, the next it's half time and then it's all over and you're on your way home.

"It's very difficult to take in until the next day when you're all over the papers."

Rob's goal helped the England team to keep an 11 match unbeaten record going for Terry Venables. He also became one of the few England internationals to score a goal in their first international match.

But it isn't all great times and Robert Lee had an especially embarrassing moment in his days at Charlton.

"We were playing against Bradford City and I got an elbow in the face and one of my contact lenses fell out. My manager, Lennie Lawrence, didn't know I wore them!

"I looked for it but of course could not find it. I didn't have any spares so I had to come off the field. The boss was not very pleased, we were 1-0 up at the time and ended up losing the game."

And players say that referees need glasses!

SAY IT AGAIN

MARTIN TYLER

"McCarthy shakes his head in agreement with the referee."

GOOD JOB HE DIDN'T
DISAGREE WITH HIM

ACTION REPLAYS

football fanatical
Steve Barlow

Railway Days

"Up the Alex!"

There's only one League ground where you'll hear that cry from the home supporters, and that's Gresty Road, home of Crewe Alexander FC. Named after a visiting princess (royalty don't drop into Crewe every day of the week), the Alex are one of the oldest League clubs; but while the likes of Wimbledon have chosen to scramble up football's social ladder to become the dodgy neighbours of the Premiership, the Alex have stayed doggedly close to their roots in the Third Division (North), remaining snugly in the lower reaches of the League.

"There was nothing very romantic about football in the lower divisions thirty years ago when I was a regular on the terraces. Crewe's ground was quite neat and cosy compared to many clubs; there was Edgeley Park, Stockport, like a collection of giant rusting bike sheds (it still is). On the Rochdale ground, at Spotland, the kids used to climb over the fence and have a kick about in the goal at half time. The gigantic unroofed bowl of the Shay at Halifax (shared with a speedway) was swept by lazy winds ('lazy' because they couldn't be bothered to go round, they just blew through you).

"Yet there were compensations. For one thing, you could and did mingle with visiting supporters and swap jokes and insults all through the game, and nobody got beaten up, unless it was a grudge match against Port Vale. After the toss, you could make your way to the end the Alex were attacking, and at the interval you could trudge past the line of blokes having a half time pee

Action Replays

against the (understandably) rusty corrugated iron fence to the other end of the ground, so you could be at the business end for both halves.

"Football's bargain basement was full of players who made up in character what they lacked in skill, and the Alex had their fair share.

"My favourite player was the goalie, Willie Mailey. Wee Wullie was a tiny Scot. Rumour had it that when scientists wanted to illustrate books on evolution with drawings of Neanderthal Man, they would write and ask for Willie's photograph.

"Being about four foot six inches tall with his studs on, Wullie was useless on crosses; to compensate for this, Crewe had a gigantic half back line to deal with the high balls. Wullie had other qualities. He was tremendously agile, and was also the bravest player I've ever seen. Diving at opponents' feet was a Mailey speciality. If an opponent dared to enter the penalty box with the ball at his feet, Wullie would sprint out of goal, there would be one of those explosions of arms and legs you get when people fight in comics, and Wullie would emerge, shake his head a couple of times, and punt the ball upfield, leaving the unfortunate forward groaning in the mud until the St John's Ambulance stretchered him off. After a couple of seasons of this, most visiting clubs adopted a policy of shooting from range at Gresty Road.

"Besides Wullie, visiting forwards ran the risk of being marked (usually for life) by Mick 'Chopper' Gannon, a half-back who bit not only your legs but your bum as well. His 10 yard sliding tackles were feared throughout the Fourth Division. He also fancied himself as a bit of a striker. His shooting was certainly ferocious, but sadly, totally inaccurate. When he shot at the Railway End goal, the ball would generally soar over the fence and a new one would have to be provided; in fact, the goalie was in the safest position for miles around, certainly safer than the

ACTION REPLAYS

passengers of any southbound train that happened to be passing behind the ground when Chopper was having a crack at the net.

"There were others. Geoff Archer, an old pro who couldn't run or tackle but who could do things with a dead ball that could make brave defenders weep; Alan Tarbuck, cousin of comedian Jimmy, who later payed for New Zealand (though to be fair, a wombat could've got a game for New Zealand in those days, if it'd had its own boots). And the ones who went on to make it big; John Mahoney, later of Stoke City and Wales; Bill Dearden, Sheffield United and England. Long after my time (though after a few pints I'll distinctly remember seeing him in a Crewe shirt) Rob Jones, Liverpool and England. We had some bloke called David Platt at one time who looked quite promising; I wonder what happened to him?

"The best match was a nail-biting cup game against Barnsley (can't remember the year) when the lead seemed to change hands every five minutes and Bill Dearden almost scored with an amazing overhead kick in the last minute that just crept past the post leaving the game a draw, 3-3.

"But my Action Replay has to be this:

"There was a spectator at Crewe, I never knew his name but everybody called him Al Teeth. He was an ugly, smelly little man with teeth like an organ keyboard who wore a pork pie hat and a dirty mac, and every home game he'd stand on the terraces at the Gresty end and hurl an incessant stream of foul abuse at the visiting team, the ref, and the Alex too when they went behind. He had a voice like an opera singer; even when we'd just scored you could hear Al Teeth yelling, 'About ****ing time!' above all the celebrations. Nothing was ever good enough for Al Teeth.

"One Saturday, he'd been having a real go at Chopper Gannon who'd been having a rotten match. His roars of scorn had been echoing round the ground for about an hour when Chopper got the ball just in front of our opponents' goal. He was steadying himself for a shot when Al Teeth's voice screamed out, 'I bet you

Action Replays

****ing miss it, you big useless ****er!'

"*I'm sure Chopper, if you asked him, would say he genuinely went for goal; what his shot actually did was scream past the post and hit Al Teeth smack in the face, lifting him off his feet and back into the arms of the spectators behind him, who cheered like anything.*

"*It could've been an accident; myself, I reckon it was the most accurate shot Chopper ever hit.*"

SAD FACT

Crewe Alexander are the least successful current football League club. They have played well over 3,100 League games without having won a major trophy!

SAY IT AGAIN
GARY LINEKER

"*You're either very good or very bad. There's no in between. We were in between.*"

BUT YOU JUST SAID THAT...OH IT DOESN'T MATTER...

TERRY BUTCHER

Action Replays Factfile

Born
December 28 1959
in Singapore

Action Replays

Clubs

Ipswich (1976-86)
Rangers (1986-90)
Coventry (1990-92) Player/manager
Sunderland (1993) Manager

Honours

1978 FA Cup
1980 First England cap v Australia
1981 UEFA Cup
1987 Scottish League Cup
1986-87 Scottish League Championship
1988 Scottish League Cup
1988-89 Scottish League Championship
1989 Scottish League Cup
1989-90 Scottish League Championship
77 England caps

ACTION REPLAYS

What character, what stature, what a patriot, what a player! So Bobby Robson, the England manager, described Terry Butcher during the Italia 1990 World Cup campaign.

A hard central defender, Butcher played for many years for Ipswich in the English League before Graeme Souness, the manager of Glasgow Rangers, paid a Scottish record of £725,000 in 1986 to take Terry to Scotland.

Not surprisingly, Terry's Action Replay comes from that first season with Rangers.

"My Action Replay comes from Scotland in 1987. It was a rare occasion because I actually scored a goal and it gave us the draw we needed to clinch Rangers' first title for nine years.

"It was my first season in Scotland. I'd come close to winning the League title in England with Ipswich, when we finished second to Aston Villa in 1981 and then runners up to Liverpool in 1982. So to have come so close twice to then go on and win the title in Scotland was a real magic moment for me.

"To score the goal was the icing on the cake of a momentous occasion for me. It was against Aberdeen, who had nothing to really play for apart from pride.

"The goal came from a free kick taken by the late Davie Cooper. It was thirty yards out on our left. He had such a great left foot and with a bit of eye contact I knew exactly where he was going to put it. He knew where I was going to run, there was telepathy there.

"Really it was just a question of making contact with the ball with my head. The cross was so perfect the the ball veered in to the net.

"It was strange, because there were lots of our supporters mixed in with the Aberdeen fans. You could see all our fans in the places they shouldn't have been, jumping up and down celebrating, they seemed to be everywhere.

Action Replays

"It was also pleasing because our player/manager Graham Souness had been sent off as well. We only drew 1-1 but it was good enough because our only rivals for the title, Celtic, lost at Falkirk.

"This was the one we all wanted. Coming back on the coach was tremendous. We stopped off for champagne. All the farmers on the country roads were dancing in the fields. Fans were coming onto the coach to have drinks with us, it was fantastic.

"The traffic queues were amazing, but it was the best jam I've ever been in. It was party time for us and those memories will never go for me. Football is such a passion in Scotland."

SAY IT AGAIN

KENNY DALGLISH

"As I say, if we score more goals than them then we'll win."

AND IF YOU DON'T, YOU WON'T...

Terry also played a major role in England, reaching the semi-finals of the 1990 World Cup in Italy. In the qualifying phase of the tournament whilst playing a match against Sweden, Terry had to have ten stitches in a head wound during the half time interval. He played on for the second half and helped England secure a 0-0 draw that took them to Italy. He was a captain that led the team by example.

Although England lost on penalties to West Germany in the semi-final, Terry recalls that special night in Turin as another of his Action Replays.

"There is one special memory though from my England career: the World Cup semi-final against Germany in Italy in 1990. I

ACTION REPLAYS

was captain; to lead your country in a World Cup semi-final, wow! It's what any man would want to do!

"That moment standing in the Turin stadium with the National Anthem was the ultimate thrill. But you needed to be concentrating on what you were about to do, namely play a very important game of football. You're thinking about your first tackle, first header and first marking job. It's only afterwards that you can sit down and reflect on what you've done.

"It's only then people tell you how much it meant to them. Even now all these years on I get told about the parties that went on during that World Cup, how people were wearing their lucky jackets and that sort of thing. It was such a thrill to have had that responsibility."

SAY IT AGAIN
BRIAN MOORE

"After a goalless first half, the score at half-time is 0-0."

YES, IT WOULD BE...

football fanatical
Garry Richardson
BBC Radio reporter, also reporter for Football Focus and Match of the Day.

GO ON SON, 'OPPIT!

ACTION REPLAYS

Garry Richardson has a job that hundreds would probably die for. He travels thousands of miles a year to report on football matches for TV and radio – and gets paid for it! He has met the greats and the not-so-greats during his career as a reporter, but he can still get excited about meeting one of the all-time great players and telling him about the best moment in his childhood!

"The moment I'll never forget was meeting my all-time hero. It seems strange to say it, but you can get blasé about interviewing footballers, because you meet so many.

"My hero was George Best. Twenty years in the job and I had never met the great man. When I was in the school playground I was George Best, and Manchester United were my team, because they'd just beaten Benfica to win the European Cup.

"Well, a short time ago I did a theatre tour with George, where I had to play the BBC interviewer asking him about his life. It was really thrilling meeting him at long, long last.

"The next day I had to drive him from Manchester to Swindon and I was really nervous about being in the car with my hero for all that time and with no one else.

"I thought what am I going to say to him...there was a real danger I would be totally tongue tied.

"So to break the ice I said to him, 'Do you remember scoring a hat trick against Southampton,' and I quoted him the year. And he said, 'Yes, I remember it well.'

"I said, 'You were substituted about nine minutes from the end,' and he remembered. He asked me how I knew, and I said 'Well I climbed over the wall and patted you on the back and was jumped on by two policemen who threw me out of the ground!'

"He thought this was hilarious, and he asked me whether I'd seen the end of the game and whether I'd got his autograph. I hadn't. But it was my best ever moment as a child, and it was wonderful to tell him the story."

Action Replays

As a reporter, Garry also gets the chance to report and tell the nation about sporting events that are happening right at that very moment!

"My favourite moments as a reporter are the rare occasions you get a story that no one else does. It's so difficult because newspapers are able to pay people for stories which we don't do at the BBC.

"But just occasionally you do get a story, and it was wonderful to be beating off the football press when Glenn Hoddle was made England manager. That was because I had got to the Chelsea director, Matthew Harding, first and he confirmed to me that Glenn had been offered the job.

"I then spent the day with Matthew because he was in close contact with Glenn while he thought over whether to take the job. It was a great feeling to be first with the news."

SAY IT AGAIN

BRYAN BUTLER

"And Keegan was there like a surgeon's knife - bang!"

HOW MANY KNIVES DO YOU KNOW THAT GO "BANG"?

CHRIS WADDLE

"It wouldn't be a surprise to see Marseille play a rough game, but it would be surprising if they did."

HEY?

CHRIS WADDLE

Action Replays Factfile

Born
December 14th 1960
in Hepworth

Action Replays

Clubs

Newcastle Utd (1980-85)

Tottenham Hotspur (1985-89)

Marseille (1989-1992)

Sheffield Wednesday (1992-)

Honours

1985 First cap for England v Eire

1989-90 French Championship

1990-91 French Championship

1991-92 French Championship

1991-92 French Cup

1993 English Footballer of the Year

62 caps for England (scored 6 goals)

ACTION REPLAYS

Chris Waddle is one of the most skilful players ever to play for England. He was once described as being: "The king of the swaying hips...the magician of the round ball." It seemed as though he could turn defenders just by looking at them and shaking his hips!

It was these skills that took him from Tottenham Hotspur to the French team, Marseille, for a staggering £4.25 million in 1989, where he became part of a very special team. The French Riviera was certainly a long way from the days when Chris worked in a sausage making factory!

"My favourite moments from my playing career came in France playing for Marseille. In particular the season 1989-90 when we won the French League. In fact I was there three seasons and we won the title in each of them, but first time round was very special.

"I'd been signed for £4.25 million which was an awful lot of money at the time. A lot of people were wondering if it was a waste of money and after a slow start I really had to prove myself to show that it was money well spent.

"People often say that a move like that sets you up for life, but to make it truly worthwhile you have to do it on the field and I was able to do so in a great team.

"It was a fantastic period for me. I had to prove to myself as a footballer that I could be the Englishman abroad on the field and adapt to continental styles. I also had to adjust to life abroad off the field as well.

"All in all it was a great challenge, I'll probably never face another one like it, unless I become manager abroad.

"I've always enjoyed Cup football, but it was winning the League which was extra special because they have to be won over 38 games as was the case in France."

Perhaps the reasons that Chris chose these League

11

Action Replays

successes are due to the fact that he has had terribly bad luck in cup competitions!

"Cups have not been too kind to me anyway. I've lost two FA Cup finals (Tottenham and Sheffield Wednesday), one Coca Cola (Sheffield Wednesday) and a couple of French Cup finals plus the 1991 European Cup final with Marseille!"

Penalty kicks are also unlucky for Chris. Unfortunately for him he will be remembered for blasting the ball over the bar in the World Cup semi-final penalty shoot out with West Germany at the 1990 World Cup! West Germany went on to win the Cup having beaten England 4-3 on penalties.

"Then there was that penalty miss in the World Cup semis in Italia 90. Everyone knows what happened, I blasted it over the bar.

"You can't print what I yelled as I saw the ball miss. Just imagine what a carpenter says when he hits his thumb with a hammer!

"That competition was still really good for England. But for a bit of luck we could have won it, and we were as good as anyone else in the tournament. We had to adjust tactics and proved that an English team could do more than just play four-four-two.

"I don't get too down after disappointments like that, and all those cup defeats. It takes a couple of days, but life goes on, and I have so many great memories. Not only at Marseille, but the early days at Newcastle and the Tottenham team that reached the Cup final in 1987 under David Pleat. We really played some great stuff that season, really lovely football.

"But it's those French titles I cherish most. I was 29-30 years of age at the time of the first one and it's great to have medals to show off."

football fanatical
Alan Green
Senior Football Commentator BBC Radio.

Action Replays

Like Garry Richardson, Alan Green watches football for a living! His is one of the most distinctive voices on the radio and if you listen to one of his commentaries, you're guaranteed to be swept along by Alan's obvious love for the game. So what is his Action Replay?

"It's very difficult to pick out a favourite moment or favourite commentary. I do between 130 and 140 games a season, spread that over ten years and that's an awful lot of games.

"I'm a very emotional commentator. I like the atmosphere of a game to take me over, to almost surf with it or swim with it, gliding along with the atmosphere. So the most emotional moments are my favourite ones.

"I felt so very low after the World Cup semi-final in Turin in 1990 when England lost on penalties. Yet that match provides me with some of my best memories.

"It's when you hear the stories afterwards. That night at Wembley, the Rolling Stones were playing. I was told that in one of the numbers there was a huge roar from the Wembley crowd. It had nothing to do with the song they were singing.

"Mick Jagger just couldn't work it out until one of the stage hands told him that Lineker had equalised. People had gone to a Rolling Stones concert with their radios to hear the football!

"So to know it had such an impact, commentating on that goal was a wonderful experience. Not because of the words I used, it was nothing special, but it's one of the few pieces of my commentary I can listen back to because I know what it meant to the listening audience, and it takes me back to the emotions I was feeling at the time.

"But my favourite moment came in the World Cup of 1982. I'd only just joined BBC Radio sport, having been a television commentator in Northern Ireland, but one of the parts of the deal that brought me to radio was that I would go to Spain to follow the Northern Irish side. I'd done all their qualifying games on the telly.

Action Replays

"Northern Ireland had a crucial game against the hosts, Spain, in Valencia. It was funny all the journalists were in their late twenties. The night before the match we all went out to a local disco. One of the organisers got us in for free. We asked her how she'd done it. She replied that she'd told the disco that we were the Northern Ireland team!

"Anyway the next day at the press conference before the game, the Spanish Press asked the Northern Ireland manager, Billy Bingham, how he felt about his team being in a disco until three in the morning the night before such a vital game.

"He said he didn't mind, it was important they had a good time. Then after the Spanish Press had gone off to do their reports Billy turned to us and said, 'What on earth have you been up to?!'"

SAY IT AGAIN
JOHN BOND

"I promise results, not promises."

SO HOW CAN YOU PROMISE THEM THEN?

"In the match, Northern Ireland were the complete underdogs. After a competitive first half, the score remained at 0-0. In the second half, a cross from Billy Hamilton was weakly pushed away by Luis Arconada, the Spanish goalkeeper. Gerry Armstrong latched on to it and struck the ball home for an incredible 1-0 lead for Northern Ireland.

"Of course Northern Ireland went on to win, to beat the hosts, Spain and top the group – unbelievable. I was commentating

Action Replays

when Armstrong scored and was absolutely overwhelmed. Then Mal Donachy was sent off, but still they hung on.

"I handed over to my colleague Peter Brackley and was then able to watch the rest of the match almost as a fan. At the end I was in tears, so proud of what my little country had achieved.

"I will never forget it because Valencia's such a passionate stadium and there I was crying my eyes out. These two Spanish fans reached over to shake my hand and that was as special a moment in football as I have ever experienced."

SAY IT AGAIN

PETER JONES

"Sporting Lisbon in their green and white hooped shirts... they look like a team of zebras"

A TEAM OF ILL ZEBRAS...

JOHN HELM

"Viv Anderson has pissed a fatness test."

WHAT CAN I SAY?!

STEVE BRUCE

Action Replays Factfile

Born
December 31st 1960
in Newcastle

Action Replays

Clubs

Gillingham (1978-84)

Norwich (1984-1987)

Manchester United (1987-1996)

Birmingham City (1996-)

Honours

1985-86 Division Two Championship

1989-90 FA Cup

1990-91 European Cup Winners Cup

1991-92 League Cup

1992-93 League Championship

1993-94 League Championship

1993-94 FA Cup

1995-96 League Championship

1995-96 FA Cup

1 B International cap for England

ACTION REPLAYS

Steve Bruce was the captain of Manchester United when they won the double of the League Championship and the FA Cup in 1994 and 1996. As the rock of the United defence along with Gary Pallister, he played a vital role in bringing glory back to Manchester United. They hadn't won the League Championship since the 1966-67 season and the previous season (1991-92) had seen them let a points advantage slip to give the Championship title to Leeds United.

In the 1992-93 season the Championship race was between Aston Villa and United. However, this time United were chasing Villa after a poor March when they went 4 matches without a win.

With this in mind, it isn't surprising that Steve Bruce has picked out a vital moment in the Championship race of the 1992-93 season.

"I would like to have a permanent Action Replay of the dying moments of Manchester United's 2-1 victory against Sheffield Wednesday in 1993."

The match took place on April 10th with United in second place and only five games to go. With the 90 minutes of the game played, Sheffield Wednesday were winning 1-0. But then up stepped Steve!

"We were losing 1-0 and the title race was very tight. Then I popped up with two goals to snatch a vital victory to take us to the top of the table, with something like five games to go."

The game was already two minutes into injury time when Dennis Irwin took a corner for United – straight into the path of Steve!

Action Replays

"The first goal came from a corner and I made a good contact and the ball soared into the roof of the net."

Remarkably the game continued and in the *seventh* minute of stoppage time, Steve's partner in the centre of defence crossed the ball. It took a deflection off a Wednesday defender and

"I got to the end of a cross, from of all people, Gary Pallister! In it went and we were top of the Premier League, when moments earlier it had looked like we were going to lose a crucial three points."

From this incredible few minutes, United never looked back and they went on to win the League for the first time in twenty-six years.

In a career with so many successes with United Steve also recalls other moments, especially the night that United beat the mighty Barcelona with 2 goals from Mark Hughes, the first of which was made by Steve with a header.

"As for other highlights, obviously lifting the Cup Winner's Cup in Rotterdam after we had beaten Barcelona in 1991, that was a great achievement. Also doing the double for the first time in 1994 was very special."

SAY IT AGAIN
GORDON LEE

"Even when you're dead you shouldn't lie down and let yourself be buried."

BUT IT COULD BE DIFFICULT TO AVOID

ACTION REPLAYS

football fanatical
Pete Taylor

Supports: Leicester City

"*I've supported Leicester City since I was a boy. I've got many memorable moments in football, but I suppose if I had to choose just one moment for my Action Replay it would be 1963 Cup final, Leicester City against Manchester United.*

"*I was lucky enough to go to several Cup finals as my dad was a senior League football referee and could get FA Cup final tickets. (I also remember vividly the 1961 final when Leicester were beaten 2-0 by Tottenham who became the first team in the 20th century to win the League and Cup double). However, the 1963 final was a special match for me for two reasons: firstly, because I'd been to see Leicester play in every round of the Cup that year and secondly, we were playing Manchester United, one of the greatest teams in the world. They also had my childhood hero playing for them – Bobby Charlton.*

"*I was 14 at the time and my dad and me took the train from Leicester down to Wembley. We got to the ground early (about 1 o'clock) because we wanted to stand at the crash barriers behind the goal. My ticket cost 4s and 6d (23p) and I remember it was blue – the Leicester colours (although they played in white that day). We took a flask of tea and our sandwiches and waited for the crowd to build and the teams to come out.*

"*Whenever I went to a match with my dad, I would always glance up at him to see how he was looking. If he looked as though we'd win, we would. I'd concentrate on his face to see any slight indication of worry or concern. Occasionally he'd look down, see me staring and give me a nod as if to say 'It's okay son, we'll win this one.' I suppose I needed reassurance from him – checking that everything was alright.*

Action Replays

"Surprisingly, in the '63 final, Leicester City were the favourites to win the Cup. They'd finished in 4th place in the First Division, just 9 points behind champions Everton, whilst United had just avoided relegation by 3 points to finish in 19th position.

"The match was a tense affair. Noel Cantwell, the United captain nearly scored an own goal early on when he headed a simple cross towards the United goal.

"Then Denis Law took over. He'd been bought for a record fee of £115,000 from the Italian club Torino by Matt Busby, the United manager at the beginning of the season. He scored the first goal after 30 minutes and mesmerised the Leicester defence with his attacking qualities. Even Gordon Banks, the great Leicester and England keeper, made errors in the match as United's David Herd scored twice in the second half. Leicester could only reply once.

"Ken Keyworth scored for Leicester with a diving header. We were behind the goal he scored in: it was the best goal of the day. But it wasn't enough.

"I remember crying as United lifted the trophy and my dad putting his arm around me to console me.

"On the train home it was fairly quiet. I remember my dad saying something like 'You've got to learn to cope with it when they lose,' which helped.

"Nevertheless, it was a great day out."

SAY IT AGAIN

JACK CHARLTON

"If in winning the game we only finish with a draw we would be fine."

SORRY, JACK?

ANDY TOWNSEND

Action Replays Factfile

**Born
July 23rd 1963
in Maidstone**

Action Replays

Clubs
Southampton (1985-88)
Norwich (1988-1990)
Chelsea (1990-1993)
Aston Villa (1993-)

Honours
1989 First cap for the Republic of Ireland (Eire) against France
1994 League Cup
1996 League Cup

ACTION REPLAYS

Andy Townsend has won over 50 caps for his country and his Action Replay comes from an international match that involved the dreaded penalty shoot out competition.

"The time that stands out most is without doubt, the penalty shoot out the Republic of Ireland had against Romania in the 1990 World Cup finals in Italy.
"The 1990 World Cup was a wonderful campaign and came at a relatively early stage in my international career. I'd been in the team for just over a year having almost come into the team by the back door. (Townsend was actually born in England, but had relatives from Eire.)"

The Republic had qualified for the second round of the World Cup after finishing second to England in qualifying group F. They had managed three draws against England, Holland and Egypt and now faced Romania who had finished 2nd in group B.

Both Romania and the Republic had near misses during a tense and closely fought match, but neither side could break the deadlock and so the match went into extra time. An extra thirty minutes was still not enough time for either side to score and so the match went to the dreaded penalty shoot out competition. Each side would nominate five players to take a penalty. If the score remained the same after the five had taken their penalties, then it would go to sudden death. Andy Townsend was one of the nominated Irish penalty takers.

"We were going first and knew that our prize would be the greatest – to play the hosts Italy in Rome in the quarter-finals. Pavarotti, the Pope and all!
"I took our third spot kick and the relief was unbelievable

Action Replays

when I hammered it home. I can't really remember what was going through my mind at the time, but I always have a golden rule: never change your mind. If you do that, you're bound to be in trouble. Decide what you're going to do and do it; after all, the shoot out business is either hit or miss. Fortunately on that occasion I hit! When that kick against Romania came up I was nervous, but I still felt good inside and the keeper helped because he went the wrong way."

With the Irish penalty takers all being successful and one of the Romanians missing a penalty, it all came down to David O'Leary who stepped up to take the vital penalty – if he scored, the Republic were through.

"David O'Leary slotted home the winning kick and I remember we went mad, all diving into a heap!"

Unfortunately, the Irish were beaten in the quarter final, 1-0 by the Italians, but nevertheless came away with great credit.

With the debate about penalty shoot outs in the news after England lost to West Germany in the semi-final of Euro '96, Andy Townsend has an insight into the situation and especially towards Gareth Southgate who missed the sudden death penalty for England.

"It can be so cruel, just as it was for my Aston Villa team mate and good friend, Gareth Southgate in Euro '96. Mind you, to go sixth is far more difficult; it's sudden death then, one miss and...

"Gareth popped round soon after the tournament and we talked it through. You just can't blame him, some people are very good penalty takers but they can still miss."

ACTION REPLAYS

And in a career that has stretched over 450 first class matches, Andy remembers his worst moment very clearly too.

"My own worst moment came in a League match when I was playing for Norwich against Chelsea. It happened in open play when I took the ball around their goalie, Dave Beasant. Just as I went to put the ball into the biggest open goal you could imagine, I took my eye off it. The ball somehow hit my heel and hit my standing leg and then went straight into Dave's arms. He just laughed at me! But I had the last laugh, we won 2-0!"

SAY IT AGAIN

KEVIN KEEGAN

"I don't think they're as good as they are."

SO HOW GOOD ARE THEY?

DEBBIE BAMPTON

Action Replays Factfile

Born
October 7th 1961

ACTION REPLAYS

Clubs

Wimbledon (1991-92)

Arsenal (1992-94)

Croydon (Player/manager) (1994-)

Honours

1977 Won first cap for England against Holland

Captain of England ladies football team

87 caps

Action Replays

"As a football fan my favourite moment has to be the climax to the League title in 1989. I'm an Arsenal fan, so when Michael Thomas scored his last minute goal against Liverpool at Anfield, it was just fantastic. It was made even better because I was away with the England team at the time. There weren't too many Arsenal fans around me at the time, but I remember one of my team-mates who's a West Ham fan, actually getting behind the Gunners that night. It must have been because she's a Southerner too!

"I'd also like a permanent Action Replay of David Linighan's goal in the last minute of extra time in the FA Cup final replay against Sheffield Wednesday in 1993. Pretty poor game, but what a great moment.

"The replay came about after a 1-1 draw in the original final. The replay was also a 1-1 draw after 90 minutes: Ian Wright having scored for Arsenal, only to see Chris Waddle send the match into extra time. As the match headed towards penalties, Andy Linighan headed a winner in the very last minute to give Arsenal a unique double victory: they'd also beaten Wednesday a few weeks previously in the League Cup final."

Debbie's Action Replay comes from her own career. Having spent most of her career with Arsenal, she took over as player/manager of Croydon WFC.

"The highlight came last season when I became the first player/manager to do the double. It was fantastic for Croydon.

"We had to play six League games in the last two weeks of the season. It all came down to our last match of the season, which we had to win. And who was it against? You've guessed it: my old club, Arsenal! We won the match and clinched the League title.

"That victory will always be with me, as will our cup final win that season over Liverpool. The match finished 1-1 but we won 4-

ACTION REPLAYS

3 on penalties to win the double. In fact we did the treble, because we also won the Surrey County Cup."

Debbie's collection of 87 caps has made her the second highest capped woman player for England. She also has an Action Replay playing for England.

"I treasure the memory of winning my first cap. It was against Holland in 1977. I was just sixteen and still at school. But the feeling I got when they played the National Anthem is still the same 86 caps later!

"Playing as a sweeper these days, I don't score too many goals, but that shouldn't be an excuse. My favourite goal for England came in the early '80s. It was a header in the semi-finals of the UEFA tournament away to Denmark. It was just one of those days when you knew everything would go well. You could just tell from the atmosphere in the dressing room. It was unbelievable!"

SAY IT AGAIN
ALAN PARRY

"With the very last kick of the game, Bobby McDonald scored with a header."

TEACH THIS MAN ANATOMY

Action Replays

football fanatical
John Heath
Supports Burnley

John Heath is a well known character in Leicester. He is a fishmonger on Leicester market and also runs an excellent fish restaurant! He was also involved in youth football for many years and was the founder and chairman of Aylestone Park Juniors – Gary Lineker's junior club.

"I was the founder of Aylestone Park Juniors. My dad loved youth football – he'd go anywhere to watch a youth match and I suppose that set me off as well. The reason that I supported Burnley was because they had a superb youth scouting policy. They created great players especially under their manager, Jimmy Adamson in the '60s. Team after team of youth players were produced – it's a role that I suppose Crewe Alexandra have taken over now.

"I've always been interested in promoting youth football – there's a great feeling about helping young players to develop, not only as footballers, but as people.

"Perhaps my proudest and greatest Action Replay concerns Gary Lineker and the first time he wore an England shirt and played in front of an England manager.

"As chairman of Aylestone Park, I'd set up a project to try and get floodlights for our club. We had lots of fund raising events and managed to raise the £1,500 needed to get the lights set up. It doesn't sound a lot nowadays, but it was in the early 70s, especially for a youth team to try and get hold of.

"We managed to scrounge six columns off the local council and twisted the arm of the street lighting company to help us get materials at cost price. A local company, Thorn Lighting, also helped out with lights and technical advice. It was unbelievable

ACTION REPLAYS

– incredible to get it all set up.

"The grand opening night for the floodlights was magical. It happened on November 4th 1974. The lights were turned on by the England manager of the time, Don Revie. The match was played between Aylestone Park Juniors and a specially selected side from the Leicester area.

"The sponsors of the England kit at the time were Admiral and they donated a set of England replica shirts to be worn by the Aylestone Park players. In our side was a special 13-year-old. His name? Gary Lineker!

"We played the match and won 4-1. I remember Gary scored – his first goal in an England shirt in front of an England manager! (He was to score a few more in the following years!) Don Revie said afterwards that he thought that several of our side could go on to higher things (in fact 5 of that team went on to become professional footballers). A funny thing was that Don Revie didn't actually pick out Gary!

"I was so proud that night. We were seeing the beginning of an era in football that night – floodlights for youth teams to help develop youth policy. I suppose we were forerunners. It was great!"

SIR BOBBY CHARLTON

Action Replays Factfile

**Born
October 11th 1937
in Ashington,
County Durham**

ACTION REPLAYS

Clubs

Manchester United (1954-73)
Preston North End (1973-75) Player/Manager
Manchester United (1975-) Director

Honours

1955-56 League Championship
1956-57 League Championship
1958 First cap for England against Scotland. Won 4-0 (Scored on debut)
1963 FA Cup
1964-65 League Championship
1966 World Cup Winners Medal
1966 English Footballer of the Year
1966 European Footballer of the Year
1966-67 League Championship
1968 European Champions
1994 Knighted

Won 106 caps for England
England's all time leading goalscorer with 49 goals (1 more than Gary Lineker)

Action Replays

Bobby Charlton is probably the most famous English footballer in the world. Just the mention of his name is enough to conjure up memories of great footballing moments: the 1966 World Cup, thunderous shots, winning the European Cup etc, etc, etc!

Football was in the Charlton blood – Bobby and his brother Jack were nephews of the Newcastle great, Jackie Milburn. Both went on to become the most famous brothers in world football.

Bobby was signed by Manchester United at the age of seventeen. He became one of the Busby Babes – the name given to the young Manchester United players managed by Matt Busby. The side won the League Championship two years running in the 1955-56 and 1956-57 seasons, setting English football alight with its flair and brilliance. However, disaster struck on February 6th 1958. United were returning from a European Cup quarter-final when the plane in which they were travelling crashed in the snow and ice at Munich airport. Twenty three passengers died including 8 of the Busby Babes. Bobby Charlton was one of the survivors. And he made the very best of that survival, going on to give people great pleasure throughout the rest of his career.

Hundreds of books and articles have been written about Charlton's achievements during his playing career because there have been so many! Understandably, having had a career that saw him gain winners medals in the greatest competitions, Sir Bobby has real problems picking out his Action Replay!

"There are just so many wonderful memories, it is very, very difficult to single any of them out. Obviously 1966 and winning the World Cup was the biggest, but then again winning the European Cup was another marvellous moment. I like to look

ACTION REPLAYS

back at the way I played and won in an international team and a club side."

It is probably such modest understatement that has helped to make Bobby Charlton one of the greatest ambassadors of the English game. His part in helping England in winning the World Cup and Manchester United becoming the first English side to win the European Cup were immeasurable. In the World Cup campaign of 1966, Charlton scored a thunderbolt goal against Mexico to help England finish top of the group in their qualifying matches. A 1-0 quarter-final victory against Argentina gave England a place in the semi-final against Portugal. To many, this match was Charlton's greatest game for England. He scored twice in an England 2-1 victory and put the legendary Portuguese player, Eusebio, into the shade with his fantastic play to give England their place in the final against West Germany.

The final at Wembley on July 30th 1966, remains the most controversial of all World Cup finals. The Germans scored first but England came back through Geoff Hurst and Martin Peters to give England a 2-1 lead. Then in the last minute of normal time, the Germans were awarded a dubious free kick. From the resulting cross, Weber scored to put the game into extra time.

The period of extra time belonged to England. Alf Ramsey, the England manager, had told his players that they had beaten the Germans once and all they had to do was to do it again. "Look at them. They're finished." He was right. A controversial Geoff Hurst goal that hit the cross bar and bounced back out was awarded and with the last kick of the match Bobby Moore, the England captain, put Hurst through to finish the match with his third goal.

Two years later on May 29th 1968, Bobby Charlton was back at Wembley in a final. This time it was with

Action Replays

Manchester United and the occasion was the European Cup final.

Charlton was captain of a United side that included George Best, Nobby Stiles and another Munich survivor, Bill Foulkes. They faced Benfica, the champions of Portugal, who included in their team an old rival of Charlton's, Eusebio. It was Charlton who scored first blood with a rare headed goal after 53 minutes. However, with just 15 minutes left, Benfica equalised and in the dying seconds of normal time Eusebio burst though the United defence and bore down on Alex Stepney, the United keeper. Instead of chipping it over Stepney or putting it wide of him, Eusebio blasted it from 18 yards. Stepney somehow managed to get his fingertips to the shot and tip it over the bar. Eusebio applauded the reflex save.

As in the World Cup final extra time was needed and like the '66 final, the English team realised that the opposition were tired. United took their opportunity and ran riot. George Best scored an incredible solo run goal, Brian Kidd scored on his nineteenth birthday and Bobby Charlton wrapped it all up with his second goal in the 104th minute of the match. As the final whistle blew, Charlton collapsed and burst into tears. United had become the first English side to win the European Cup.

Charlton simply said of the night:

"I remember all my honours with great affection. But it was more than that, it helped ease the memory of that Munich night ten years previously."

As a director of United, Bobby Charlton is proud of the recent success of the club. Incredibly, it has a parallel with his own era of the Busby Babes, in the sense that many of today's United stars are home grown products and the

ACTION REPLAYS

manager is an uncompromising Scot, who wants to develop the best players at his club. As Charlton says:

"I get great pleasure from seeing the crop of United youngsters. It's just wonderful to see them winning the titles and the cups that they've achieved over the past few seasons. It doesn't eclipse my playing days, they're entirely separate, but as a director at United I have to derive great satisfaction from seeing the current team do well."

SAY IT AGAIN

JOHN BARRETT

"We don't always get from slow motion the pace at which they play."

WELL OF COURSE YOU WOULDN'T

TONY ADAMS

Action Replays Factfile

**Born
October 10th 1966
in Romford**

ACTION REPLAYS

Club
Arsenal (1983-   )

Honours
1986-87 PFA Young Player of the Year

1987 League Cup

1987 First cap for England against Spain

1988-89 League Championship

1990-91 League Championship

1993 League Cup

1993 FA Cup

1994 European Cup Winners Cup

Action Replays

Tony Adams is one of the most solid defenders of his generation. As captain of Arsenal, he has led them to success in several competitions and established the Arsenal defence as one of the most solid in the League. He has also achieved international recognition and captained England. It is these two parts to his career that provide his Action Replays.

"I can pick Action Replays from both my Arsenal and England careers. The Arsenal one is easy:1989 and winning the League title and taking it to Highbury for the first time in ages.

"It was the manner we did it in, with Michael Thomas scoring our all important goal against Liverpool at Anfield."

The match that decided the 1988-89 League Championship took place at Anfield on May 26th. Liverpool were top of the table, Arsenal were second, three points behind. All Liverpool had to do to win the title was to win or draw. They could even afford to be defeated by one goal and so win the double (they'd already won the Cup 6 days earlier). However a 2-0 win for Arsenal would give the Highbury team the title for the first time in 18 years. It was that close! The first half saw both sides play at an incredible pace. Both managers had made tactical decisions to try and stop the other side gaining the upper hand and at half time the match stood at 0-0. Then seven minutes into the second half, Alan Smith scored for Arsenal. 1-0 to the Gunners!

As the minutes ticked away, it looked as though Liverpool were going to succeed in winning the double. The match went into injury time and 40,000 Liverpool fans whistled like crazy to try and get the referee to blow for time. However, Arsenal weren't quite finished. Defender, Lee Dixon cleared the ball to Alan Smith who pushed it into the path of Arsenal's midfield dynamo, Michael Thomas. He

ACTION REPLAYS

avoided two challenges, waited for the Liverpool keeper, Bruce Grobbelaar, to commit himself then flicked the ball into the Liverpool goal. 2-0 Arsenal! The referee blew for full time and the title was Arsenal's! Never before had the League title been decided with the last kick of the last match of the season! Tony remembers the drama of the occasion.

"It's very hard to recall what I was feeling up to the point that the goal was scored because so much goes through your mind. But then when the ball went in, it was just amazing. I don't think anything that dramatic will ever happen again. I was captain that night and I can't put into words what it felt like to receive the trophy."

Tony has won over 40 England caps and has also captained the side. He is justly proud of his international career.

"As for England, I was so proud to win my first cap. It came in 1987 against Spain and we won 4-2. Gary Lineker scored all four of our goals and it was a very special night. Then to captain my country, it's everyone's dream. I couldn't imagine it would happen to me. I did it for the first time against Romania in 1994. It was a 1-1 draw and Rob Lee scored on his debut."

But what about the Euro '96 competition in which England reached the semi-finals, only to be beaten by Germany on penalties? Tony was the England captain for the campaign, so was this a highlight for him?

"There are no truly special memories from leading England in Euro '96. Such feelings would be irrelevant, totally irrelevant because ultimately we didn't succeed. The press got so excited, but people didn't realise it wasn't special for me because we failed. I'm a winner!"

Action Replays

Such a determined attitude exactly fits George Graham's description of his former captain.

"One of the game's great characters."

SAY IT AGAIN

PETER JONES

"Well, it's Ipswich 0, Liverpool 2, and if that's the way the score stays then you've got to fancy Liverpool to win."

WELL YOU WOULD WOULDN'T YOU?

RAY STUBBS

"A late consolation goal for Middlesborough - they won't take any consolation from that."

SO IT'S NOT MUCH OF A CONSOLATION THEN, IS IT?

ACTION REPLAYS

football fanatical
Iain Carter

Supports: Leicester City

"I'm not a very good footballer. I can't tell you how hard it is to say that, particularly after so many great individual moments in a playing career that stretches twenty or so years.

"It's true though – far more losses than wins.

"That's despite scoring goals direct from corners twice (Overdale Juniors and Lancaster Boys School). Only one of those was a goal keeping error as well, and that was the wind assisted one!

"Then there were the mazey runs, one, two, three, four outstretched legs beaten as I went from box to box on a mud heap; what a goal that would've been...

"Or when I took up goalkeeping, the penalty save on my debut for Sullivans Fives in the South London League. I dived to my right, he hit it straight and it hit my legs. Great save though.

"But there's the rub; what about the one that went through my legs, the pass back that wasn't anticipated, the shot from the halfway line that wasn't seen? As I say, far more losses than wins. I've had enough of finishing bottom, I'm packing up.

"Perhaps it's appropriate that I support Leicester City, the team that regularly bobs from Premiership to Division One with exhilarating and disappointing regularity, depending on the season. Every triumph means that there's a disaster waiting to happen.

"I'm not a very good supporter. I watch them when I can and always want them to win. There've been so many disappointments though, so I'm prone to be very critical of them.

"I won't be now, not now they've given me the moment for my Action Replay. You can keep the penalty saves, goals from corners and the mazey runs that end in disappointment because my legs

are too tired to shoot properly...just forget them.

"Remember Steve Claridge in the 1996 play off final between Leicester and Crystal Palace at Wembley? The shinner that soared into the Crystal Palace net in the last minute of extra time. I swear it was an Action Replay when it happened. It was like slow motion, the ball sailing from his swinging shin on the edge of the area, Nigel Martyn the Palace keeper, stranded, a packed Wembley held in silent awe and then the euphoric crescendo of noise.

"And so Leicester City are back in the Premiership. Goals that result in wins like that don't happen in my football life. Maybe it's a change of fortune, maybe we're going to stay up for more than a season.

"Now where did I put those keepers' gloves, or should I try outfield again?"

Do you have a favourite Action Replay?
Write to the authors
c/o Piccadilly Press 5 Castle Rd, London NW1 8PR.
Please remember to include your full name and address.

SAY IT AGAIN
TREVOR BROOKING

"If only he'd chanced his arm with his left leg."

HE'D HAVE BEEN CONFUSED

THE ANORAK SECTION

WHO OR WHAT ARE ANORAKS?

Anorak: *(Noun) A strange breed of people who remember the most obscure facts in the world.* Anoraks *can be found in all sections of society, but are especially abundant amongst followers of all sports. (These people are not to be confused with trainspotters, who are totally saddo cases!)*

ARE YOU A FOOTBALLING ANORAK?

Try these top ten anorak questions to find out if YOU are suffering symptoms of anorakism!

1) When was the corner kick introduced into football's rules?

2) In which year did the crossbar replace a length of tape?

3) Which English player was once a sausage seasoning maker?

4) Who scored the fastest ever goal for England in an international?

5) How long did Bill Lambton last as Scunthorpe United's manager in 1959?

6) How many games did Ray Wilcox play for Newport County without scoring a goal?

7) How near to the sea is Arbroath's football ground?

8) Why is Aberdeen's ground called Pittodrie?

9) When was the first football match played under floodlights?

Action Replays

10) Who were the first brothers to play in the same FA Cup final team?

SAY IT AGAIN
PETER JONES

"Lawrenson slipped the ball through to Williams, and he beat Shilton from 35 yards... and you don't beat Shilton from 35 yards."

BUT I THOUGHT YOU SAID HE JUST DID?

1) 1872
2) 1875
3) *Chris Waddle*
4) *Tommy Lawton in 17 seconds against Portugal in 1947*
5) *3 days*
6) 489 *(his total career!)*
7) *50 yards*
8) *It is built on a former dung heap and Pittodrie is Celtic for place of manure.*
9) *October 1878 in Sheffield*
10) *Hubert and Frederick Heron for Wanderers and Hon. Alfred and Hon. Rev Edward Lyttleton for Old Etonians in the 1876 Cup Final*

THE ANORAK SECTION

If you got at least one question right we're afraid you have early symptoms of anorakism.

If you got several of these questions right, then you are without doubt, an anorak and should attempt to get out more and meet fellow human beings!

If you got them all right you are beyond all known cures! You are the grade 1, numero uno, League champion, ANORAK OF THE UNIVERSE (complete with big woolly hood!)

SAY IT AGAIN

ANDY SMITH:

So at the end of the day, why do you think Arsenal won?

GEORGE GRAHAM:

Because we scored 2 goals and Sheffield Wednesday scored 1.

THANK YOU, MR GRAHAM

PS If you actually looked up any of the answers, then you are very sad and should realise that there is more to life than looking up the answers to irrelevant trivial questions! (This makes the writers of this book more than totally sad because they had to look up the questions!)

However, just in case you wish to develop anorak tendencies, this section of the book will help you out. Within the following pages are results stretching back to the beginning of football.

Amaze your friends, worry your parents, sit back and read THE ANORAK section!

Action Replays

WEIRD FACTS

HOW MANY?

The highest win in a first class British match happened on 12 September 1885. In the first round of the Scottish Cup Arbroath beat Bon Accord 36-0!

Arbroath also "scored" another seven times, but these were disallowed for offside! John Petrie scored 13 of the goals, a British record for most goals in a first class game.

The highest International win by a British side was achieved by England who beat beat Ireland 13-0 in 1882!

The highest win in the FA Cup happened in 1887 when Preston North End beat Hyde United 26-0 in the first round.

Drayton Grange Colts beat Eldon Sports Reserves 49-0 in 1988. Even Drayton Grange's goalie scored!

Courage Colts Under 14s scored first in their match against Midas FC Under 14s. They needn't have bothered, because Midas then scored 59 goals to win 59-1!

I'D RATHER NOT REMEMBER THAT, THANK YOU!

Pat Kruse of Torquay United holds a record he would rather not have. In a 1977 League match between Torquay and Cambridge, he managed to head the ball into his own goal after only 6 seconds to record the fastest ever own goal scored in a first class match.

Kevin Moran is still the only player to have been sent off in an FA Cup final. He was playing for Manchester United against Everton in the 1985 final.

THE ANORAK SECTION

The fastest ever sending off in a first class match was achieved by Mark Smith of Crewe Alexander. He received his marching orders in a 1994 match against Darlington after only 19 seconds!

The fastest sending off in a World Cup match is held by Uruguay's Jose Batista. He was sent off after 55 seconds in a 1986 match against Scotland.

The club who have had most players sent off in one match is Hereford United. They had 4 of their men sent off in a division 3 match against Northampton Town in 1992.

Bill Lambton holds the record for the shortest reign as a Football League manager. In 1959 he was in charge of Scunthorpe United for the grand total of 3 days! (The longest reign as a Football League manager was by Fred Everiss who was in charge of West Bromwich Albion between 1902-48 A total of 46 years!)

Feel sorry for vale of Leven who didn't win at all during the 1891-92 season in Scotland.

HOW LONG?

The longest unbeaten sequence in British football was achieved by Nottingham Forest. They went 42 games without defeat between November 1977-December 1978.

The longest unbeaten at home sequence goes to Liverpool. They went 85 games without being beaten at Anfield between January 1978-January 1981.

Liverpool also hold the longest unbeaten cup sequence in

Action Replays

British football. They went 25 rounds without defeat in the League/Milk Cup between 1980-84.

The longest unbeaten start to a season is shared between Leeds United who went 29 games without defeat at the beginning of the 1973-74 season and Liverpool who equalled this achievement at the start of the 1987-88 season. Both went on to win the title.

When Arsenal won the First Division title in 1990-91 they only lost 1 out of the 38 League games played.

Dixie Dean of Everton holds the longest sequence of scoring in consecutive matches. He scored 23 in 12 games in the 1930-31 season. He also holds the record of most goals in a season. In the 1927-28 season he scored 60 for Everton.

Arthur Rowley holds the record for most goals scored in a career. Between 1946-1965 he scored 434 goals in 619 games.

In Scotland, Jimmy McGory scored 410 goals in 408 games in a career that lasted from 1922-38.

Joe Pane of Luton scored 10 goals in a Division 3 South match against Bristol Rovers in 1936.

Goalkeeper Chris Woods of Rangers holds the British record for keeping a clean sheet, not letting in a goal. He went 1196 minutes without letting in a goal from 26 November 1986 to 31 January 1987.

Paul Cooper of Ipswich Town saved 8 out of 10 penalties he faced during the 1979-80 season.

THE ANORAK SECTION

RESULTS

WORLD CUP

The idea for a football World Cup was conceived by two Frenchmen, Jules Rimet and Henry Delaunay, in 1904. However, it took 26 years for the idea to grow into reality.

It wasn't until 1930 in Uruguay that the first World Cup took place, with 13 teams competing for the 30 cm high gold Jules Rimet trophy.

From such a small beginning the World Cup finals have grown into being perhaps the greatest sporting occasion in the world with over two billion people watching the 1994 final.

URUGUAY 1930

Pool 1

France	4	Mexico	1
Argentina	1	France	0
Chile	3	Mexico	0
Chile	1	France	0
Argentina	6	Mexico	3
Argentina	3	Chile	1

	P	W	D	L	F	A	Pts
Argentina	3	3	0	0	10	4	6
Chile	3	2	0	1	5	3	4
France	3	1	0	2	4	3	2
Mexico	3	0	0	3	4	13	0

Pool 2

Yugoslavia	2	Brazil	1
Yugoslavia	4	Bolivia	0
Brazil	4	Bolivia	0

	P	W	D	L	F	A	Pts
Yugoslavia	2	2	0	0	6	1	4
Brazil	2	1	0	1	5	2	2
Bolivia	2	0	0	2	0	8	0

Pool 3

Romania	3	Peru	1
Uruguay	1	Peru	0
Uruguay	4	Romania	0

	P	W	D	L	F	A	Pts
Uruguay	2	2	0	0	5	0	4
Romania	2	1	0	1	3	5	2
Peru	2	0	0	2	1	4	0

Pool 4

USA	3	Belgium	0
USA	3	Paraguay	0
Paraguay	1	Belgium	0

	P	W	D	L	F	A	Pts
USA	2	2	0	0	6	0	4
Paraguay	2	1	0	1	1	3	2
Belgium	2	0	0	2	0	4	0

Semi-finals

Argentina	6	USA	1
Uruguay	6	Yugoslavia	1

Final

Uruguay	4	Argentina	2

AET: After Extra Time
R: Replay

Action Replays

Leading Scorers
Stabile (Argentina) 8
Cea (Uruguay) 5

ITALY 1934

First Round
Italy	7	USA	1
Czech.	2	Romania	1
Germany	5	Belgium	2
Austria	3	France	2
Spain	3	Brazil	1
Switzerland	3	Holland	2
Sweden	3	Argentina	2
Hungary	4	Egypt	2

Second Round
Germany	2	Sweden	1
Austria	2	Hungary	1
Italy	1	Spain	1(AET)
Italy	1	Spain	0 (R)
Czech.	3	Switzerland	2

Semi-finals
| Czech. | 3 | Germany | 1 |
| Italy | 1 | Austria | 0 |

Third Place Match
Germany 3 Austria 2

Final
Italy 2 Czech. 1(AET)

Leading Scorers
Nejedly(Czechoslovakia) 4
Schiavo (Italy) 4
Conen (Germany) 4

FRANCE 1938

First round
Switzerland	1	Germany	1(AET)
Switzerland	4	Germany	2 (R)
Cuba	3	Romania	3(AET)
Cuba	2	Romania	1 (R)
Hungary	6	Dutch E.Ind.	0
France	3	Belgium	1
Czech.	3	Holland	0
Brazil	6	Poland	5 (AET)
Italy	2	Norway	1 (AET)

Second Round
Sweden	8	Cuba	0
Hungary	2	Switzerland	0
Italy	3	France	1
Brazil	1	Czech.	1 (AET)
Brazil	2	Czech.	1 (R)

Semi-finals
| Italy | 2 | Brazil | 1 |
| Hungary | 5 | Sweden | 1 |

Third Place Match
Brazil 4 Sweden 2

Final
Italy 4 Hungary 2

Leading Scorers
Leonidas (Brazil) 8
Szengeller (Hungary) 7
Piola (Italy) 5

BRAZIL 1950

First Round

Pool 1
Brazil	4	Mexico	0
Yugoslavia	3	Switzerland	0
Yugoslavia	4	Mexico	1
Brazil	2	Switzerland	2
Brazil	2	Yugoslavia	0
Switzerland	2	Mexico	1

	P	W	D	L	F	A	Pts
Brazil	3	2	1	0	8	2	5
Yugoslavia	3	2	0	1	7	3	4
Switzerland	3	1	1	1	4	6	3
Mexico	3	0	0	3	2	10	0

84

THE ANORAK SECTION

Pool 2
Spain	3	USA	0
England	2	Chile	0
USA	1	England	0
Chile	5	USA	2
Spain	1	England	0

	P	W	D	L	F	A	Pts
Spain	3	3	0	0	6	1	6
England	3	1	0	2	2	2	2
Chile	3	1	0	2	5	6	2
USA	3	1	0	2	4	8	2

Pool 3
Sweden	3	Italy	2
Sweden	2	Paraguay	2
Italy	2	Paraguay	0

	P	W	D	L	F	A	Pts
Sweden	2	2	0	5	4	3	
Italy	2	1	0	1	4	3	2
Paraguay	2	0	1	1	2	4	1

Pool 4
Uruguay	8	Bolivia	0

	P	W	D	L	F	A	Pts
Uruguay	1	1	0	0	8	0	2
Bolivia	1	0	0	1	0	8	0

Final Pool
Uruguay	2	Spain	2
Brazil	7	Sweden	1
Uruguay	3	Sweden	2
Brazil	6	Spain	1
Sweden	3	Spain	1
Uruguay	2	Brazil	1

	P	W	D	L	F	A	Pts
Uruguay	3	2	1	0	7	5	5
Brazil	3	2	0	1	14	4	4
Sweden	3	1	0	2	6	11	2
Spain	3	0	1	2	4	11	1

Winners
Uruguay

Leading Scorers
Ademir (Brazil)	9
Schiaffino (Uruguay)	6
Zarra (Spain)	5

SAY IT AGAIN
GRAHAM TAYLOR

"Well, I think Arsenal will either win or lose the championship this year."

THE EX-MANAGER OF ENGLAND
SHOWING GREAT INSIGHT

SWITZERLAND 1954

Pool 1
Yugoslavia	1	France	0
Brazil	5	Mexico	0
France	3	Mexico	2
Brazil	1	Yugoslavia	1

	P	W	D	L	F	A	Pts
Brazil	2	1	1	0	6	1	3
Yugoslavia	2	1	1	0	2	1	3
France	2	1	0	1	3	3	2
Mexico	2	0	0	2	2	8	0

Pool 2
Hungary	9	Korea	0
W. Germany	4	Turkey	1
Hungary	8	W.Germany	3
Turkey	7	Korea	0

	P	W	D	L	F	A	Pts
Hungary	2	2	0	0	17	3	4
W. Germany	2	1	0	1	7	9	2
Turkey	2	1	0	1	8	4	2
Korea	2	0	0	2	0	16	0

Action Replays

Play-off
W. Germany 7   Turkey   2

Pool 3
Austria   1   Scotland   0
Uruguay   2   Czech.   0
Austria   5   Czech.   0
Uruguay   7   Scotland   0

	P	W	D	L	F	A	Pts
Uruguay	2	2	0	0	9	0	4
Austria	2	2	0	0	6	0	4
Czech.	2	0	0	2	0	7	0
Scotland	2	0	0	2	0	8	0

Pool 4
England   4   Belgium   4
England   2   Switzerland   0
Switzerland   2   Italy   1
Italy   4   Belgium   1

	P	W	D	L	F	A	Pts
England	2	1	1	0	6	4	3
Italy	2	1	0	1	5	3	2
Switzerland	2	1	0	1	2	3	2
Belgium	2	0	1	1	5	8	1

Play-off
Switzerland   4   Italy   1

Quarter-finals
W. Germany   2   Yugoslavia   0
Hungary   4   Brazil   2
Austria   7   Switzerland   5
Uruguay   4   England   2

Semi-finals
W. Germany   6   Austria   1
Hungary   4   Uruguay   2

Third Place Match
Austria   3   Uruguay   1

Final
W. Germany   3   Hungary   2

Leading Scorers
Kocsis (Hungary)   11
Morlock (W. Germany)   8
Probst (Austria)   6
Hugi (Switzerland)   6

SAY IT AGAIN
ROY McFARLAND

"We've got to sit down and have a think about where we stand."

INTERESTING BODY POSITION THAT ONE!

SWEDEN 1954

W. Germany   3   Argentina   1
N.Ireland   1   Czech.   0
W. Germany   2   Czech.   2
Argentina   3   N.Ireland   1
W. Germany   2   N.Ireland   2
Czech.   6   Argentina   1

	P	W	D	L	F	A	Pts
W. Germany	3	1	2	0	7	5	4
Czech.	3	1	1	1	8	4	3
N.Ireland	3	1	1	1	4	5	3
Argentina	3	1	0	2	5	10	2

Play-off
N.Ireland   2   Czech.   1

Pool 2
France   7   Paraguay   3
Yugoslavia   1   Scotland   1
Yugoslavia   3   France   2
Paraguay   3   Scotland   2
France   2   Scotland   1
Yugoslavia   3   Paraguay   3

THE ANORAK SECTION

	P	W	D	L	F	A	Pts
France	3	2	0	1	11	7	4
Yugoslavia	3	1	2	0	7	6	4
Paraguay	3	1	1	1	9	12	3
Scotland	3	0	1	2	4	6	1

Pool 3
Sweden	3	Mexico	0
Hungary	1	Wales	1
Wales	1	Mexico	1
Sweden	2	Hungary	1
Sweden	0	Wales	0
Hungary	4	Mexico	0

	P	W	D	L	F	A	Pts
Sweden	3	2	1	0	5	1	5
Hungary	3	1	1	1	6	3	3
Wales	3	0	3	0	2	2	3
Mexico	3	0	1	2	1	8	1

Play-off
| Wales | 2 | Hungary | 1 |

Pool 4
England	2	Sovt. Union	2
Brazil	3	Austria	0
England	0	Brazil	0
Sovt. Union	2	Austria	0
Brazil	2	Sovt. Union	0
England	2	Austria	2

	P	W	D	L	F	A	Pts
Brazil	3	2	1	0	5	0	5
England	3	0	3	0	4	4	3
Sovt. Union	3	1	1	1	4	4	3
Austria	3	0	1	2	2	7	1

Play-off
| Sovt. Union | 1 | England | 0 |

Quarter-finals
France	4	N.Ireland	0
W. Germany	1	Yugoslavia	0
Sweden	2	Sovt. Union	0
Brazil	1	Wales	0

Semi-finals
| Brazil | 5 | France | 2 |
| Sweden | 3 | W. Germany | 1 |

Third Place Match
| France | 6 | W. Germany | 3 |

Final
| Brazil | 5 | Sweden | 2 |

Leading Scorers
Fontaine (France)	13
Pele (Brazil)	6
Rahn (W. Germany)	6

CHILE 1962

Group 1
Uruguay	2	Colombia	1
Sovt. Union	2	Yugoslavia	0
Yugoslavia	3	Uruguay	1
Sovt. Union	4	Colombia	4
Sovt. Union	2	Uruguay	1
Yugoslavia	5	Colombia	0

	P	W	D	L	F	A	Pts
Sovt. Union	3	2	1	0	8	5	5
Yugoslavia	3	2	0	1	8	3	4
Uruguay	3	1	0	2	4	6	2
Colombia	3	0	1	2	5	11	1

Group 2
Chile	3	Switzerland	1
W. Germany	0	Italy	0
Chile	2	Italy	0
W. Germany	2	Switzerland	0
W. Germany	2	Chile	0
Italy	3	Switzerland	0

	P	W	D	L	F	A	Pts
W. Germany	3	2	1	0	4	1	5
Chile	3	2	0	1	5	3	4
Italy	3	1	1	1	3	2	3
Switzerland	3	0	0	3	2	8	0

Action Replays

Group 3
Brazil	2	Mexico	0
Czech.	1	Spain	0
Brazil	0	Czech.	0
Spain	1	Mexico	0
Brazil	2	Spain	1
Mexico	3	Czech.	1

	P	W	D	L	F	A	Pts
Brazil	3	2	1	0	4	1	5
Czech.	3	1	1	1	2	3	3
Mexico	3	1	0	2	2	3	2
Spain	3	1	0	2	2	3	2

Group 4
Argentina	1	Bulgaria	0
Hungary	2	England	1
England	3	Argentina	1
Hungary	6	Bulgaria	1
Argentina	0	Hungary	0
England	0	Bulgaria	0

	P	W	D	L	F	A	Pts
Hungary	3	2	1	0	8	2	5
England	3	1	1	1	4	3	3
Argentina	3	1	1	1	2	3	3
Bulgaria	3	0	1	2	1	7	1

Quarter-finals
Yugoslavia	1	W. Germany	0
Brazil	3	England	1
Chile	2	Sovt. Union	1
Czech.	1	Hungary	0

Semi-finals
Brazil	4	Chile	2
Czech.	3	Yugoslavia	1

Third Place Match
Chile	1	Yugoslavia	0

Final
Brazil	3	Czech.	1

Leading Scorers
- Garrincha (Brazil) 4
- Vava (Brazil) 4
- L. Sanchez (Chile) 4
- Jerkovic (Yugoslavia) 4
- Albert (Hungary) 4

ENGLAND 1066

Group 1
England	0	Uruguay	0
France	1	Mexico	1
Uruguay	2	France	1
England	2	Mexico	0
Uruguay	0	Mexico	0
England	2	France	0

	P	W	D	L	F	A	Pts
England	3	2	1	0	4	0	5
Uruguay	3	1	2	0	2	1	4
Mexico	3	0	2	1	1	3	2
France	3	0	1	2	2	5	1

Group 2
W. Germany	5	Switzerland	0
Argentina	2	Spain	1
Spain	2	Switzerland	1
Argentina	0	W. Germany	0
Argentina	2	Switzerland	0
W. Germany	2	Spain	1

	P	W	D	L	F	A	Pts
W. Germany	3	2	1	0	7	1	5
Argentina	3	2	1	0	4	1	5
Spain	3	1	0	2	4	5	2
Switzerland	3	0	0	3	1	9	0

Group 3
Brazil	2	Bulgaria	0
Portugal	3	Hungary	1
Hungary	3	Brazil	1
Portugal	3	Bulgaria	0
Portugal	3	Brazil	1
Hungary	3	Bulgaria	1

THE ANORAK SECTION

	P	W	D	L	F	A	Pts
Portugal	3	3	0	0	9	2	6
Hungary	3	2	0	1	7	5	4
Brazil	3	1	0	2	4	6	2
Bulgaria	3	0	0	3	1	8	0

Group 4
Sovt. Union	3	North Korea	0
Italy	2	Chile	0
Chile	1	North Korea	1
Sovt. Union	1	Italy	0
North Korea	1	Italy	0
Sovt. Union	2	Chile	1

	P	W	D	L	F	A	Pts
Sovt. Union	3	3	0	0	6	1	6
North Korea	3	1	1	1	2	4	3
Italy	3	1	0	2	2	2	2
Chile	3	0	1	2	2	5	1

Quarter-finals
England	1	Argentina	0
W. Germany	4	Uruguay	0
Portugal	5	North Korea	3
Sovt. Union	2	Hungary	1

Semi-finals
W. Germany	2	Sovt. Union	1
England	2	Portugal	1

Third Place Match
Portugal	2	Sovt. Union	1

Final
England	4	Germany	2(AET)

Leading Scorers
Eusebio (Portugal)	9
Haller (W. Germany)	5
Beckenbauer (W. Germany)	4
Hurst (England)	4
Bene (Hungary)	4
Porkujan (Sovt. Union)	4

SAY IT AGAIN
DEREK JOHNSTONE

"And who can forget that memorable match last time between these sides, when I think the score was four-three..."

THAT MEMORABLE, HEY?

MEXICO 1970

Group 1
Mexico	0	Sovt. Union	0
Belgium	3	El Salvador	0
Sovt. Union	4	Belgium	1
Mexico	4	El Salvador	0
Sovt. Union	2	El Salvador	0
Mexico	1	Belgium	0

	P	W	D	L	F	A	Pts
Sovt. Union	3	2	1	0	6	1	5
Mexico	3	2	1	0	5	0	5
Belgium	3	1	0	2	4	5	2
El Salvador	3	0	0	3	0	9	0

Group 2
Uruguay	2	Israel	0
Italy	1	Sweden	0
Uruguay	0	Italy	0
Sweden	1	Israel	1
Sweden	1	Uruguay	1
Italy	1	Israel	0

	P	W	D	L	F	A	Pts
Italy	3	1	2	0	1	0	4
Uruguay	3	1	1	1	2	1	3
Sweden	3	1	1	1	2	2	3
Israel	3	0	2	1	1	3	2

Action Replays

Group 3
England	1	Romania	0
Brazil	4	Czech.	1
Romania	2	Czech.	1
Brazil	1	England	0
Brazil	3	Romania	2
England	1	Czech.	0

	P	W	D	L	F	A	Pts
Brazil	3	3	0	0	8	3	6
England	3	2	0	1	2	1	4
Romania	3	1	0	2	4	5	2
Czech.	3	0	0	3	2	7	0

Group 4
Peru	3	Bulgaria	2
W. Germany	2	Morocco	1
Peru	3	Morocco	0
W. Germany	5	Bulgaria	2
W. Germany	3	Peru	1
Morocco	1	Bulgaria	1

	P	W	D	L	F	A	Pts
W. Germany	3	3	0	0	10	4	6
Peru	3	2	0	1	7	5	4
Bulgaria	3	0	1	2	5	9	1
Morocco	3	0	1	2	2	6	1

Quarter-finals
W. Germany	3	England	2(AET)
Brazil	4	Peru	2
Italy	4	Mexico	1
Uruguay	1	Sovt.Union	0

Semi-finals
Italy	4	W.Germany	3(AET)
Brazil	3	Uruguay	1

Third Place Match
W. Germany	1	Uruguay	0

Final
Brazil	4	Italy	1

Leading Scorers
Muller (W. Germany)	9
Jairzinho (Brazil)	7

WEST GERMANY 1974

Group 1
W. Germany	1	Chile	0
E. Germany	2	Australia	0
W. Germany	3	Australia	0
E. Germany	1	Chile	1
E. Germany	1	W. Germany	0
Chile	0	Australia	0

	P	W	D	L	F	A	Pts
E. Germany	3	2	1	0	4	1	5
W. Germany	3	2	0	1	4	1	4
Chile	3	0	2	1	1	2	1
Australia	3	0	1	2	0	5	1

Group 2
Brazil	0	Yugoslavia	0
Scotland	2	Zaire	0
Brazil	0	Scotland	0
Yugoslavia	9	Zaire	0
Scotland	1	Yugoslavia	1
Brazil	3	Zaire	0

	P	W	D	L	F	A	Pts
Yugoslavia	3	1	2	0	10	1	4
Brazil	3	1	2	0	3	0	4
Scotland	3	1	2	0	3	1	4
Zaire	3	0	0	3	0	14	0

Group 3
Holland	2	Uruguay	0
Sweden	0	Bulgaria	0
Holland	0	Sweden	0
Bulgaria	1	Uruguay	1
Holland	4	Bulgaria	1
Sweden	3	Uruguay	0

	P	W	D	L	F	A	Pts
Holland	3	2	1	0	6	1	5
Sweden	3	1	2	0	3	0	4

THE ANORAK SECTION

| Bulgaria | 3 | 0 | 2 | 1 | 2 | 5 | 2 |
| Uruguay | 3 | 0 | 1 | 2 | 1 | 6 | 1 |

Group 4
Italy	3	Haiti	1
Poland	3	Argentina	2
Italy	1	Argentina	1
Poland	7	Haiti	0
Argentina	4	Haiti	1
Poland	2	Italy	1

	P	W	D	L	F	A	Pts
Poland	3	3	0	0	12	3	6
Argentina	3	1	1	1	7	5	3
Italy	3	1	1	1	5	4	3
Haiti	3	0	0	3	2	14	0

Group A
Brazil	1	E. Germany	0
Holland	4	Argentina	0
Holland	2	E. Germany	0
Brazil	2	Argentina	1
Holland	2	Brazil	0
Argentina	1	E. Germany	1

	P	W	D	L	F	A	Pts
Holland	3	3	0	0	8	0	6
Brazil	3	2	0	1	3	3	4
E.Germany	3	0	1	2	1	4	1
Argentina	3	0	1	2	2	7	1

Group B
Poland	1	Sweden	0
W. Germany	2	Yugoslavia	0
Poland	2	Yugoslavia	1
W. Germany	4	Sweden	2
Sweden	2	Yugoslavia	1
W. Germany	1	Poland	0

	P	W	D	L	F	A	Pts
W. Germany	3	3	0	0	7	2	6
Poland	3	2	0	1	3	2	4
Sweden	3	1	0	2	4	6	2
Yugoslavia	3	0	0	3	2	6	0

Third Place Match
Poland 1 Brazil 0

Final
W. Germany 2 Holland 1

Leading Scorers
Lato (Poland) 7
Neeskens (Holland) 5
Szarmach (Poland) 5

1978 ARGENTINA

Group 1
Argentina	2	Hungary	1
Italy	2	France	1
Argentina	2	France	1
Italy	3	Hungary	1
Italy	1	Argentina	0
France	3	Hungary	1

	P	W	D	L	F	A	Pts
Italy	3	3	0	0	6	2	6
Argentina	3	2	0	1	4	3	4
France	3	1	0	2	5	5	2
Hungary	3	0	0	3	3	8	0

Group 2
W. Germany	0	Poland	0
Tunisia	3	Mexico	1
Poland	1	Tunisia	0
W. Germany	6	Mexico	0
Poland	3	Mexico	1
W. Germany	0	Tunisia	0

	P	W	D	L	F	A	Pts
Poland	3	2	1	0	4	1	5
W. Germany	3	1	2	0	6	0	4
Tunisia	3	1	1	1	3	2	3
Mexico	3	0	0	3	2	12	0

Group 3
Austria	2	Spain	1
Sweden	1	Brazil	1
Austria	1	Sweden	0

91

Action Replays

Brazil	0	Spain	0
Spain	1	Sweden	0
Brazil	1	Austria	0

	P	W	D	L	F	A	Pts
Austria	3	2	0	1	3	2	4
Brazil	3	1	2	0	2	1	4
Spain	3	1	1	1	2	2	3
Sweden	3	0	1	2	1	3	1

Group 4
Peru	3	Scotland	1
Holland	3	Iran	1
Scotland	1	Iran	1
Holland	0	Peru	0
Peru	4	Iran	1
Scotland	3	Holland	2

	P	W	D	L	F	A	Pts
Peru	3	2	1	0	7	2	5
Holland	3	1	1	1	5	3	3
Scotland	3	1	1	1	5	6	3
Iran	3	0	1	2	2	8	1

Group A
Italy	0	W. Germany	0
Holland	5	Austria	1
Italy	1	Austria	0
Austria	3	W. Germany	2
Holland	2	Italy	1
Holland	2	W. Germany	2

	P	W	D	L	F	A	Pts
Holland	3	2	1	0	9	4	5
Italy	3	1	1	1	2	2	3
W. Germany	3	0	2	1	4	5	2
Austria	3	1	0	2	4	8	2

Group B
Argentina	2	Poland	0
Brazil	3	Peru	0
Argentina	0	Brazil	0
Poland	1	Peru	0
Brazil	3	Poland	1
Argentina	6	Peru	0

	P	W	D	L	F	A	Pts
Argentina	3	2	1	0	8	0	5
Brazil	3	2	1	0	6	1	5
Poland	3	1	0	2	2	5	2
Peru	3	0	0	3	0	10	0

Third Place Match
Brazil 2 Italy 1

Final
Argentina 3 Holland 1 (AET)

Leading Scorers
Kempes (Argentina) 6
Rensenbrink (Holland) 5
Cubillas (Peru) 5

1982 SPAIN

Group 1
Italy	0	Poland	0
Peru	0	Cameroon	0
Italy	1	Peru	1
Poland	0	Cameroon	0
Poland	5	Peru	1
Italy	1	Cameroon	1

	P	W	D	L	F	A	Pts
Poland	3	1	2	0	5	1	4
Italy	3	0	3	0	2	2	3
Cameroon	3	0	3	0	1	1	3
Peru	3	0	2	1	2	6	2

Group 2
Algeria	2	W. Germany	1
Austria	1	Chile	0
W. Germany	4	Chile	1
Austria	2	Algeria	1
Algeria	3	Chile	2
W. Germany	1	Austria	0

	P	W	D	L	F	A	Pts
W. Germany	3	2	0	1	6	3	4
Austria	3	2	0	1	3	1	4
Algeria	3	2	0	1	5	5	4
Chile	3	0	0	3	3	8	0

THE ANORAK SECTION

Group 3
Belgium	1	Argentina	0
Hungary	10	El Salvador	1
Argentina	4	Hungary	1
Belgium	1	El Salvador	0
Belgium	1	Hungary	1
Argentina	2	El Salvador	0

	P	W	D	L	F	A	Pts
Belgium	3	2	1	0	3	1	5
Argentina	3	2	0	1	6	2	4
Hungary	3	1	1	1	12	6	3
El Salvador	3	0	0	3	1	13	3

SAY IT AGAIN

ELTON WELSBY:
"Magnifique, Eric."

ERIC CANTONA:
"Oh, do you speak French?"

ELTON WELSBY:
"Non."

OOH LA LA!

Group 4
England	3	France	1
Czech.	1	Kuwait	1
England	2	Czech.	0
France	4	Kuwait	1
France	1	Czech.	1
England	1	Kuwait	1

	P	W	D	L	F	A	Pts
England	3	3	0	0	6	1	6
France	3	1	1	1	6	5	3
Czech.	3	0	2	1	2	4	2
Kuwait	3	0	1	2	2	6	1

Group 5
Spain	1	Honduras	1
N.Ireland	0	Yugoslavia	0
Spain	2	Yugoslavia	1
N.Ireland	1	Honduras	1
Yugoslavia	1	Honduras	0
N.Ireland	1	Spain	0

	P	W	D	L	F	A	Pts
N.Ireland	3	1	2	0	2	1	4
Spain	3	1	1	1	3	3	3
Yugoslavia	3	1	1	1	2	2	3
Honduras	3	0	2	1	2	3	2

Group 6
Brazil	2	Sovt. Union	1
Scotland	5	N. Zealand	2
Brazil	4	Scotland	1
Sovt. Union	3	N. Zealand	0
Scotland	2	Sovt. Union	2
Brazil	4	N. Zealand	0

	P	W	D	L	F	A	Pts
Brazil	3	3	0	0	10	2	6
Sovt. Union	3	1	1	1	6	4	3
Scotland	3	1	1	1	8	8	3
N. Zealand	3	0	0	3	2	12	0

Group A
Poland	3	Belgium	0
Sovt. Union	1	Belgium	0
Sovt. Union	0	Poland	0

	P	W	D	L	F	A	Pts
Poland	2	1	1	0	3	0	3
Sovt. Union	2	1	1	0	1	0	3
Belgium	2	0	0	2	0	4	0

Group B
W. Germany	0	England	0
W. Germany	2	Spain	1
England	0	Spain	0

	P	W	D	L	F	A	Pts
W. Germany	2	1	1	0	2	1	3
England	2	0	2	0	0	0	2
Spain	2	0	1	1	1	2	1

Action Replays

Group C
Italy	2	Argentina	1
Brazil	3	Argentina	1
Italy	3	Brazil	2

	P	W	D	L	F	A	Pts
Italy	2	2	0	0	5	3	4
Brazil	2	1	0	1	5	4	2
Argentina	2	0	0	2	2	5	0

Group D
France	1	Austria	0
N.Ireland	2	Austria	2
France	4	N.Ireland	1

	P	W	D	L	F	A	Pts
France	2	2	0	0	5	1	4
Austria	2	0	1	1	2	3	1
N.Ireland	2	0	1	1	3	6	1

Semi-finals
Italy	2	Poland	0
W. Germany	3	France 3 (AET)	

West Germany won 5-4 on penalties

Third Place Match
Poland	3	France	2

Final
Italy	3	W. Germany	1

Leading Scorers
- Rossi (Italy) 6
- Rummenigge (W. Germany) 5
- Zico (Brazil) 4
- Boniek (Poland) 4

MEXICO 1986

Group A
Bulgaria	1	Italy	1
Argentina	3	S. Korea	1
Italy	1	Argentina	1
Bulgaria	1	S. Korea	1
Argentina	2	Bulgaria	0
Italy	3	S. Korea	2

SAY IT AGAIN
BRIAN LITTLE

"We could easily go out and spend £40,000 on a player, but that, of course, is impossible."

BUT I THOUGHT YOU SAID IT WAS EASY?

	P	W	D	L	F	A	Pts
Argentina	3	2	1	0	6	2	5
Italy	3	1	2	0	5	4	4
Bulgaria	3	0	2	1	2	4	2
S. Korea	3	0	1	2	4	7	1

Group B
Mexico	2	Belgium	1
Paraguay	1	Iraq	0
Mexico	1	Paraguay	1
Belgium	2	Iraq	1
Paraguay	2	Belgium	2
Mexico	1	Iraq	0

	P	W	D	L	F	A	Pts
Mexico	3	2	1	0	4	2	5
Paraguay	3	1	2	0	4	3	4
Belgium	3	1	1	1	5	5	4
Iraq	3	0	0	3	1	4	0

Group C
Sovt. Union	6	Hungary	0
France	1	Canada	0
Sovt. Union	1	France	1
Hungary	2	Canada	0
France	3	Hungary	0
Sovt. Union	2	Canada	0

	P	W	D	L	F	A	Pts
Sovt. Union	3	2	1	0	9	1	5
France	3	2	1	0	5	1	5

THE ANORAK SECTION

| Hungary | 3 | 1 | 0 | 2 | 2 | 9 | 2 |
| Canada | 3 | 0 | 0 | 3 | 0 | 5 | 0 |

Group D
Brazil	1	Spain	0
N.Ireland	1	Algeria	1
Spain	2	N.Ireland	1
Brazil	1	Algeria	0
Spain	3	Algeria	0
Brazil	3	N.Ireland	0

	P	W	D	L	F	A	Pts
Brazil	3	3	0	0	5	0	6
Spain	3	2	0	1	5	2	4
N.Ireland	3	0	1	2	2	6	1
Algeria	3	0	1	2	1	5	1

Group E
W. Germany	1	Uruguay	1
Denmark	1	Scotland	0
Denmark	6	Uruguay	1
W. Germany	2	Scotland	1
Scotland	0	Uruguay	0
Denmark	2	W. Germany	0

	P	W	D	L	F	A	Pts
Denmark	3	3	0	0	9	1	6
W. Germany	3	1	1	1	3	4	3
Uruguay	3	0	2	1	2	7	2
Scotland	3	0	1	2	1	3	1

Group F
Morocco	0	Poland	0
Portugal	1	England	0
England	0	Morocco	0
Poland	1	Portugal	0
England	3	Poland	0
Morocco	3	Portugal	1

	P	W	D	L	F	A	Pts
Morocco	3	1	2	0	3	1	4
England	3	1	1	1	3	1	3
Poland	3	1	1	1	1	3	3
Portugal	3	1	0	2	2	4	2

Second Round
A knock-out phase consisting of the top two teams from each group plus the four best third-placed teams

Brazil	4	Poland	0
Argentina	1	Uruguay	0
Mexico	2	Bulgaria	0
Belgium	4	Sovt. Union	3 (AET)
France	2	Italy	0
W. Germany	1	Morocco	0
England	3	Paraguay	0
Spain	5	Denmark	1

Quarter-finals
| France | 1 | Brazil | 1 (AET) |

France won 4-3 on penalties

| W. Germany | 0 | Mexico | 0 (AET) |

West Germany won 4-1 on penalties

| Argentina | 2 | England | 1 |
| Belgium | 1 | Spain | 1 (AET) |

Belgium won 5-4 on penalties

Semi-finals
| Argentina | 2 | Belgium | 0 |
| W. Germany | 2 | France | 0 |

Third Place Match
| France | 4 | Belgium | 2 |

Final
| Argentina | 3 | W. Germany | 2 |

Leading Scorers
Lineker (England) 6
Butragueño (Spain) 5
Careca (Brazil) 5
Maradona (Argentina) 5

ITALY 1990

Group A
Italy	1	Austria	0
Czech.	5	USA	1
Italy	1	USA	0

95

Action Replays

Czech.	1	Austria	0
Italy	2	Czech.	0
Austria	2	USA	1

SAY IT AGAIN
ALEX FERGUSON

"You don't get any bigger than the quarter-finals of the FA Cup."

APART FROM THE SEMI FINALS, THE FINAL, THE WORLD CUP, ETC ETC

	P	W	D	L	F	A	Pts
Italy	3	3	0	0	4	0	6
Czech.	3	2	0	1	6	3	4
Austria	3	1	0	2	2	3	2
USA	3	0	0	3	2	8	0

Group B

Cameroon	1	Argentina	0
Romania	2	Sovt. Union	0
Argentina	2	Sovt. Union	0
Cameroon	2	Romania	1
Argentina	1	Romania	1
Sovt. Union	4	Cameroon	0

	P	W	D	L	F	A	Pts
Cameroon	3	2	0	1	3	5	4
Romania	3	1	1	1	4	3	3
Argentina	3	1	1	1	3	2	3
Sovt. Union	3	1	0	2	4	4	2

Group C

Brazil	2	Sweden	1
Costa Rica	1	Scotland	0
Brazil	1	Costa Rica	0
Scotland	2	Sweden	1
Brazil	1	Scotland	0
Costa Rica	2	Sweden	1

	P	W	D	L	F	A	Pts
Brazil	3	3	0	0	4	1	6
Costa Rica	3	2	0	1	3	2	4
Scotland	3	1	0	2	2	3	2
Sweden	3	0	0	3	3	6	0

Group D

Colombia	2	UAE	0
W. Germany	1	Yugoslavia	1
Yugoslavia	1	Colombia	0
W. Germany	5	UAE	1
W. Germany	1	Colombia	1
Yugoslavia	4	UAE	1

	P	W	D	L	F	A	Pts
W. Germany	3	2	1	0	10	3	5
Yugoslavia	3	2	0	1	6	5	4
Colombia	3	1	1	1	3	2	3
UAE	3	0	0	3	2	11	0

Group E

Belgium	2	S. Korea	0
Uruguay	0	Spain	0
Belgium	3	Uruguay	1
Spain	3	S. Korea	1
Spain	2	Belgium	1
Uruguay	1	S. Korea	0

	P	W	D	L	F	A	Pts
Spain	3	2	1	0	5	2	5
Belgium	3	2	0	1	6	3	4
Uruguay	3	1	1	1	2	3	3
S. Korea	3	0	0	3	1	6	0

Group F

England	1	Rep. Ireland	1
Holland	1	Egypt	1
England	0	Holland	0
Egypt	0	Rep. Ireland	1
England	1	Egypt	0
Holland	1	Rep. Ireland	1

	P	W	D	L	F	A	Pts
England	3	1	2	0	2	1	4
Rep. Ireland	3	0	3	0	2	2	3

THE ANORAK SECTION

| Holland | 3 | 0 | 3 | 0 | 2 | 2 | 3 |
| Egypt | 3 | 0 | 2 | 1 | 1 | 2 | 2 |

Second Phase
A knock-out phase consisting of the top two teams from each group plus the four best third-placed teams

Cameroon	2	Colombia	1 (AET)
Czech.	4	Costa Rica	1
Argentina	1	Brazil	0
W. Germany	2	Holland	1
Rep. Ireland	0	Romania	0 (AET)

Republic of Ireland won 5-4 on penalties

Italy	2	Uruguay	0
Yugoslavia	2	Spain	1 (AET)
England	1	Belgium	0 (AET)

Quarter-finals
| Argentina | 0 | Yugoslavia | 0 |

Argentina won 3-2 on penalties

Italy	1	Rep. Ireland	0
W. Germany	1	Czech	0
England	3	Cameroon	2 (AET)

Semi-finals
| Argentina | 1 | Italy | 1 (AET) |

Argentina won 4-3 on penalties

| W. Germany | 1 | England | 1 (AET) |

West Germany won 4-3 on penalties

Third Place Match
| Italy | 2 | England | 1 |

Final
| W. Germany | 1 | Argentina | 0 |

Leading scorers
Schillaci (Italy)	6
Skuhravy (Czech.)	5
Michel (Spain)	4
Milla (Cameroon)	4
Matthaus (W. Germany)	4
Lineker (England)	4

USA 1994

Group A
USA	1	Switzerland	1
Romania	3	Colombia	1
USA	2	Colombia	1
Switzerland	4	Romania	1
Romania	1	USA	0
Colombia	2	Switzerland	0

	P	W	D	L	F	A	Pts
Romania	3	2	0	1	5	5	6
Switzerland	3	1	1	1	5	4	4
USA	3	1	1	1	3	3	4
Colombia	3	1	0	2	4	5	3

Group B
Cameroon	2	Sweden	2
Brazil	2	Russia	0
Brazil	3	Cameroon	0
Sweden	3	Russia	1
Russia	6	Cameroon	1
Brazil	1	Sweden	1

	P	W	D	L	F	A	Pts
Brazil	3	2	1	0	6	1	7
Sweden	3	1	2	0	6	4	5
Russia	3	1	0	2	7	6	3
Cameroon	3	0	1	2	3	11	1

Group C
Germany	1	Bolivia	0
Spain	2	S. Korea	2
Germany	1	Spain	1
S. Korea	0	Bolivia	0
Spain	3	Bolivia	1
Germany	3	S. Korea	2

	P	W	D	L	F	A	Pts
Germany	3	2	1	0	5	3	7
Spain	3	1	2	0	6	4	5
S. Korea	3	0	2	1	4	5	2
Bolivia	3	0	1	2	1	4	1

Action Replays

Group D

Argentina	4	Greece	0
Nigeria	3	Bulgaria	0
Argentina	2	Nigeria	1
Bulgaria	4	Greece	0
Nigeria	2	Greece	0
Bulgaria	2	Argentina	0

	P	W	D	L	F	A	Pts
Nigeria	3	2	0	1	6	2	6
Bulgaria	3	2	0	1	6	3	6
Argentina	3	2	0	1	6	3	6
Greece	3	0	0	3	0	10	1

Group E

Rep. Ireland	1	Italy	0
Norway	1	Mexico	0
Italy	1	Norway	0
Mexico	2	Rep. Ireland	1
Rep. Ireland	0	Norway	0
Italy	1	Mexico	1

	P	W	D	L	F	A	Pts
Mexico	3	1	1	1	3	3	4
Rep. Ireland	3	1	1	1	2	2	4
Italy	3	1	1	1	2	2	4
Norway	3	1	1	1	1	1	4

Group F

Belgium	1	Morocco	0
Holland	2	S. Arabia	1
Belgium	1	Holland	0
S. Arabia	2	Morocco	1
Holland	2	Morocco	1
S. Arabia	1	Belgium	0

	P	W	D	L	F	A	Pts
Holland	3	2	0	1	4	3	6
S. Arabia	3	2	0	1	4	3	6
Belgium	3	2	0	1	2	1	6
Morocco	3	0	0	3	2	5	0

Second Phase

A knock-out phase consisting of the top two teams from each group plus the four best third-placed teams

Germany	3	Belgium	2
Spain	3	Switzerland	0
Sweden	3	S. Arabia	1
Romania	3	Argentina	2
Holland	2	Rep. Ireland	0
Brazil	1	USA	0
Italy	2	Nigeria	1 (AET)
Bulgaria	1	Mexico	1 (AET)

Bulgaria won 3-1 on penalties

Quarter-finals

Italy	2	Spain	1
Brazil	3	Holland	2
Bulgaria	2	Germany	1
Sweden	2	Romania	2 (AET)

Sweden won 5-4 on penalties

Semi-finals

Brazil	1	Sweden	0
Italy	2	Bulgaria	1

Third Place Match

Sweden	4	Bulgaria	0

Final

Brazil	0	Italy	0

Brazil won 3-2 on penalties

Leading Scorers

Salenko (Russia)	6
Stoichkov (Bulgaria)	6
K. Andersson (Sweden)	5
R. Baggio (Italy)	5
Klinsmann (Germany)	5
Romario (Brazil)	5

THE ANORAK SECTION

EUROPEAN CHAMPIONSHIP

This is held every four years and is played for between the European member nations of FIFA.

Finals
1960 Paris
  Sovt. Union 2 Yugoslavia 1

1964 Madrid
  Spain 2 Sovt. Union 1

1968 Rome
  Italy 1 Yugoslavia 1
  Rome (R)
  Italy 2 Yugoslavia 0

1972 Brussels
  W. Germany 3 Sovt. Union 0

1976 Belgrade
  Czech. 2 W. Germany 2 (AET)
  Czechoslovakia won 5-4 on penalties

1980 Rome
  W. Germany 2 Belgium 1

1984 Paris
  France 2 Spain 0

1988 Munich
  Holland 2 Sovt. Union 0

1992 Stockholm
  Denmark 2 Germany 0

1996 London
  Germany 2 Czech. 1
  (Germany won on Golden Goal Rule AET)

COPA AMERICA SOUTH AMERICAN CHAMPIONSHIP

This is the oldest running championship in the world. It is played for by the 10 international members of CONMEBOL, the South America Confederation.

Year	Winners
1910	Argentina
1916	Uruguay
1917	Uruguay
1919	Brazil
1920	Uruguay
1921	Argentina
1922	Brazil
1923	Uruguay
1924	Uruguay
1925	Argentina
1926	Uruguay
1927	Uruguay
1929	Argentina
1935	Uruguay
1937	Argentina
1939	Peru
1941	Argentina
1942	Uruguay
1945	Argentina
1946	Argentina
1947	Argentina
1949	Brazil
1953	Paraguay
1955	Argentina
1957	Argentina
1958	Argentina
1959	Uruguay
1963	Bolivia
1967	Uruguay
1975	Peru
1979	Paraguay
1983	Uruguay
1987	Uruguay
1989	Brazil

Action Replays

1991 Argentina
1993 Argentina
1995 Uruguay

AFRICAN NATIONS CUP

This is the premier football event of African football. It is held every 2 years in a nominated country.

Finals

1957 Khartoum
 Egypt 4 Ethiopia 0

1959 Cairo
 1st Egypt 2nd Sudan

1962 Addis Ababa
 Ethiopia 4 Egypt 2 (AET)

1963 Accra
 Ghana 3 Sudan 0

1965 Tunis
 Ghana 3 Tunisia 2

1968 Addis Ababa
 Congo Kinshasha (Zaire)1 Ghana 0

1970 Khartoum
 Sudan 1 Ghana 0

1972 Yaounde
 Congo 3 Mali 2

1974 Cairo
 Zaire 2 Zambia 2
 Cairo (R)
 Zaire 2 Zambia 0

1976 Addis Ababa
 1st Morocco 2nd Guinea

1978 Accra
 Ghana 2 Algeria 0

1980 Lagos
 Nigeria 3 Algeria 0

1982 Tripoli
 Ghana 1 Libya 1 (AET)
 Ghana won 7-6 on penalties

1984 Abidjan
 Cameroon 3 Nigeria 0

1986 Cairo
 Egypt 0 Cameroon 0 (AET)
 Egypt won 5-4 on penalties

1988 Casablanca
 Cameroon 1 Nigeria 0

1990 Algiers
 Algeria 1 Nigeria 0

1992 Dakar
 Ghana 0 Ivory Coast 0 (AET)
 Ghana won 11-10 on penalties

1994 Tunis
 Nigeria 2 Zambia 1

1996
 S. Africa 2 Tunisia 0

ASIAN CUP

The Asian Cup began in 1956 and is played for by Asian member nations of FIFA

Asian Cup Finals
1956 S. Korea 2   Israel   1
1960 S. Korea 3   Israel   0
1964 Israel   2   India   0

100

THE ANORAK SECTION

1968 Iran	3	Burma	1
1972 Iran	2	South Korea	1
1976 Iran	1	Kuwait	0
1980 Kuwait	3	South Korea	0
1984 S. Arabia	2	China	0
1988 S. Arabia	0	S. Korea	0

Saudi Arabia won 4-3 on penalties

| 1992 Japan | 1 | S. Arabia | 0 |

OLYMPIC FOOTBALL

Although football has been officially part of the Olympics since 1908, it has not fitted into the Olympic ideal of amateur sport. Even in the early days there were arguments about whether payments to players could be made. From 1952 the Olympics were dominated by Eastern European teams, because they could put out full strength sides whilst claiming that their players were amateurs even though the state paid them to play football. In the 1992 Barcelona Olympics only players under the age of 23 could play. In Atlanta in 1996 the rules were changed again: although players had to be under 23 teams could include 3 over-age players.

1896 Athens*
  1 Denmark
  2 Greece

1900 Paris*
  1 Great Britain
  2 France

1904 St Louis**
  Gold Canada
  Silver USA

1908 London
  Gold England
  Silver Denmark
  Bronze Holland

1912 Stockholm
  Gold England
  Silver Denmark
  Bronze Holland

1920 Antwerp
  Gold Belgium
  Silver Spain
  Bronze Holland

1924 Paris
  Gold Uruguay
  Silver Switzerland
  Bronze Sweden

1928 Amsterdam
  Gold Uruguay
  Silver Argentina
  Bronze Italy

1932 Los Angeles
  No tournament

1936 Berlin
  Gold Italy
  Silver Austria
  Bronze Norway

1948 London
  Gold Sweden
  Silver Yugoslavia
  Bronze Denmark

1952 Helsinki
  Gold Hungary
  Silver Yugoslavia
  Bronze Sweden

1956 Melbourne
  Gold USSR
  Silver Yugoslavia
  Bronze Bulgaria

Action Replays

1960 Rome
 Gold Yugoslavia
 Silver Denmark
 Bronze Hungary

SAY IT AGAIN
DENIS LAW

"Whoever wins today will win the championship no matter who wins."

SAY THAT AGAIN!

1964 Tokyo
 Gold Hungary
 Silver Czech.
 Bronze E. Germany

1968 Mexico City
 Gold Hungary
 Silver Bulgaria
 Bronze Japan

1972 Munich
 Gold Poland
 Silver Hungary
 Bronze E. Germany/Sovt. Union

1976 Montreal
 Gold E. Germany
 Silver Poland
 Bronze USSR

1980 Moscow
 Gold Czechoslovakia
 Silver E. Germany
 Bronze Sovt. Union

1984 Los Angeles
 Gold France
 Silver Brazil
 Bronze Yugoslavia

1988 Seoul
 Gold Sovt. Union
 Silver Brazil
 Bronze W. Germany

1992 Barcelona
 Gold Spain
 Silver Poland
 Bronze Ghana

* No official tournament
** No official tournament but gold medal later awarded by IOC

CONCACAF CHAMPIONSHIP

The Central American Championship has been known as The CONCACAF Gold Cup since 1991.

Year	Winners
1941	Costa Rica
1943	El Salvador
1946	Costa Rica
1948	Costa Rica
1951	Panama
1953	Costa Rica
1955	Costa Rica
1957	Haiti
1960	Costa Rica
1961	Costa Rica
1963	Costa Rica
1965	Mexico
1967	Guatemala
1969	Costa Rica
1971	Mexico
1973	Haiti
1977	Mexico
1981	Honduras
1985	Canada

1989   Costa Rica
1991   USA
1993   Mexico
1995   Mexico

INTERNATIONAL YOUTH FOOTBALL

FIFA UNDER-20 WORLD CHAMPIONSHIP

Finals
1977
Sovt. Union   2   Mexico   2
  Sovt. Union won 9-8 on penalties
1979
Argentina   3   Sovt. Union   1
1981
W. Germany   4   Qatar   0
1983
Brazil   1   Argentina   0
1985
Brazil   1   Spain   0
1987
Yugoslavia   1   W. Germany   1
  Yugoslavia won 5-4 on penalties
1989
Portugal   2   Nigeria   0
1991
Portugal   0   Brazil   0
  Portugal won 4-2 on penalties
1993
Brazil   2   Ghana   1
1995
Argentina   2   Brazil   0

FIFA UNDER-17 WORLD CHAMPIONSHIP

Finals
1985
Nigeria   2   W. Germany   0
1987
Sovt. Union   1   Nigeria   1
  Sovt. Union won 4-2 on penalties.
1989
S. Arabia   2   Scotland   2
  S. Arabia won 5-4 on penalties
1991
Ghana   1   Spain   0
1993
Nigeria   2   Ghana   1

EUROPEAN UNDER 21 CHAMPIONSHIP

Year	Winner
1978	Yugoslavia
1980	Sovt. Union
1982	England
1984	England
1986	Spain
1988	France
1990	Sovt. Union
1992	Italy
1994	Portugal

EUROPEAN YOUTH CHAMPIONSHIP

This was called the European Junior Championship for Under 18s until 1981.

Year	Winner
1948	England
1949	France
1950	Austria
1951	Yugoslavia
1952	Spain
1953	Hungary
1954	Spain
1955	No final

1956	No final	1974	Brazil
1957	Austria	1975	Uruguay
1958	Italy	1977	Uruguay
1959	Bulgaria	1979	Uruguay
1960	Hungary	1981	Uruguay
1961	Portugal	1983	Brazil
1962	Romania	1985	Brazil
1963	England	1987	Colombia
1964	England	1988	Brazil
1965	E. Germany	1991	Brazil
1966	Sovt. Union and Italy	1993	Colombia
1967	Sovt. Union	1995	Brazil
1968	Czech.		
1969	Bulgaria		
1970	E. Germany		
1971	England		
1972	England		
1973	England		
1974	Bulgaria		
1975	England		
1976	Sovt. Union		
1977	Belgium		
1978	Sovt. Union		
1979	Yugoslavia		
1980	England		
1981	W. Germany		
1982	Scotland		
1983	France		
1984	Hungary		
1986	E. Germany		
1988	Sovt. Union		
1990	Sovt. Union		
1992	Turkey		
1993	England		

SOUTH AMERICAN YOUTH CUP

Year	Winner
1954	Uruguay
1958	Uruguay
1964	Uruguay
1967	Argentina
1971	Paraguay

SAY IT AGAIN

GRAHAM ROBERTS

*"Football's a game of skill...
we kicked them a bit and they
kicked us a bit."*

YEAH, DEAD SKILFUL!

EUROPEAN CUP

The European Champion's Club Cup is played between the champions of each European country plus the holders of the trophy.

Recent developments to the Champion's League has meant many more games on a league basis rather than a knock-out competition. It has also meant that fewer smaller countries' champions are able to take part.

Results
1956 Paris
    Real Madrid 4   Stade de Reims 3

THE ANORAK SECTION

1957 Madrid
  Real Madrid 4   Fiorentina 0

1958 Brussels
  Real Madrid 2   Milan 2 (AET)

1959 Stuttgart
  Real Madrid 2   Stade de Reims 0

1960 Glasgow
  Real Madrid 7   Eintracht Frankfurt 3

1961 Berne
  Benfica 3   Barcelona 2

1962 Amsterdam
  Benfica 5   Real Madrid 3

1963 Wembley
  Milan 2   Benfica 1

1964 Vienna
  Internazionale 3   Real Madrid 1

1965 Milan
  Internazionale 1   Benfica 0

1966 Brussels
  Real Madrid 2   Partizan Belgrade 1

1967 Lisbon
  Celtic 2   Internazionale 1

1968 Wembley
  Man. Utd 4   Benfica 1 (AET)

1969 Madrid
  Milan 4   Ajax Amsterdam 1

1970 Milan
  Feyenoord 2   Celtic 1 (AET)

1971 Wembley
  Ajax Amsterdam 2   Panathinaikos 0

1972 Rotterdam
  Ajax Amsterdam 2   Internazionale 0

1973 Belgrade
  Ajax Amsterdam 1   Juventus 0

1974 Brussels
  Bayern Munich 1   Atletico Madrid 1 (AET)

Brussels (R)
  Bayern Munich 4   Atletico Madrid 0

1975 Paris
  Bayern Munich 2   Leeds United 0

1976 Glasgow
  Bayern Munich 1   St Etienne 0

1977 Rome
  Liverpool 3   Borussia Monchengladbach 1

1978 Wembley
  Liverpool 1   Club Bruge 0

1979 Munich
  Nottingham Forest 1   Malmo 0

1980 Madrid
  Nottingham Forest 1   Hamburg 0

1981 Paris
  Liverpool 1   Real Madrid 0

1982 Rotterdam
  Aston Villa 1   Bayern Munich 0

1983 Athens
  Hamburg 1   Juventus 0

Action Replays

1984 Rome
 Liverpool 1 AS Roma 1 (AET)
 Liverpool won 4-2 on penalties

1985 Brussels
 Juventus 1 Liverpool 0

1986 Seville
 Steaua Bucharest 0
  Barcelona 0 (AET)
 Steaua Bucharest won 2-0 on penalties

1987 Vienna
 FC Porto 2 Bayern Munich 1

1988 Stuttgart
 PSV Eindhoven 0 Benfica 0 (AET)
 PSV Eindhoven won 6-5 on penalties

1989 Barcelona
 Milan 4 Steaua Bucharest 0

1990 Vienna
 Milan 1 Benfica 0

1991 Bari
 Red Star Belgrade 0 Marseille 0 (AET)
 Red Star Belgrade won 5-3 on penalties

1992 Wembley
 Barcelona 1 Sampdoria 0 (AET)

1993 Munich
 Marseille 1 Milan 0
 Marseille were stripped of the title after allegations of match fixing

1994 Athens
 Milan 4 Barcelona 0

1995 Vienna
 Ajax Amsterdam 1 Milan 0

1996 Rome
 Juventus 1
  Ajax Amsterdam 1 (AET)
 Juventus won 4-2 on penalties

EUROPEAN CUP WINNERS CUP

Played between the winners of European nations national knock-out competitions.

1961 Glasgow
 Rangers 0 Fiorentina 2

Florence
 Fiorentina 2 Rangers 1
 Fiorentina won 4-1 on aggregate

1962 Glasgow
 Atletico Madrid 1 Fiorentina 1 (AET)
 Stuttgart (R)
 Atletico Madrid 3 Fiorentina 0

1963 Rotterdam.
 Tottenham Hotspur 5
  Atletico Madrid 1

1964 Brussels
 Sporting Lisbon 3
  MTK Budapest 3 (AET)

Antwerp (R)
 Sporting Lisbon 1 MTK Budapest 0

1965 Wembley
 West Ham U 2
  TSV Munich 1860 0

1966 Glasgow
 Borussia Dortmund 2
  Liverpool 1 (AET)

1967 Nuremberg
 Bayern Munich 1 Rangers 0 (AET)

THE ANORAK SECTION

1968 Rotterdam
 Milan 2   Hamburg SV 0

1969 Basle
 Slovan Bratislava 3   Barcelona 2

1970 Vienna
 Manchester City 2   Gornik Zabrze 1

1971 Athens
 Chelsea 1   Real Madrid 1 (AET)
Athens (R)
 Chelsea 2   Real Madrid 1

1972 Barcelona
 Rangers 3   Moscow Dynamo 2

1973 Salonika
 Milan 1   Leeds United 0

1974 Rotterdam
 FC Magdeburg 2   Milan 0

1975 Basle
 Kiev Dynamo 3   Ferencvaros 0

1976 Brussels
 Anderlecht 4   West Ham United 2

1977 Amsterdam
 Hamburg SV 2   Anderlecht 0

1978 Paris
 Anderlecht 4   FK Austria 0

1979 Basle
 Barcelona 4
           Fortuna Dusseldorf 3 (AET)

1980 Brussels
 Valencia 0   Arsenal 0 (AET)
 Valencia won 5-4 on penalties

1981 Dusseldorf
 Dynamo Tbilisi 2 Carl Zeiss Jena 1

1982 Barcelona
 Barcelona 2   Standard Liege 1

1983 Gothenburg
 Aberdeen 2   Real Madrid 1(AET)

1984 Basle
 Juventus 2   FC Porto 1

1985 Rotterdam
 Everton 3   Rapid Vienna 1

1986 Lyons
 Kiev Dynamo 3   Atletico Madrid 0

1987 Athens
 Ajax Amsterdam 1
           Lokomotive Leipzig 0

1988 Strasbourg
 Mechelen 1   Ajax Amsterdam 0

1989 Berne
 Barcelona 2   Sampdoria 0

1990 Gothenburg
 Sampdoria 2   Anderlecht 0 (AET)

1991 Rotterdam
 Man. Utd 2   Barcelona 1

1992 Lisbon
 Werder Bremen 2   Monaco 0

1993 Wembley
 Parma 3   Antwerp 1

1994 Copenhagen
 Arsenal 1   Parma 0

1995 Paris
 Real Zaragoza 2   Arsenal 1

1996 Brussels
 Paris St Germain 1   Rapid Vienna 0

107

UEFA CUP

This was called the Fairs Cup until 1972 and was originally a competition designed to give meaning to friendly matches played between cities holding trade fairs at the time.

It is now contested between European clubs with each country being allowed a certain number of entries based on past European performances.

1958 London
  London Select XI 2   Barcelona 2
Barcelona
  Barcelona 6   London Select XI 0
  Winners: Barcelona, 8-2 on aggregate

1960 Birmingham
  Birmingham City 0   Barcelona 0
Barcelona
  Barcelona 4   Birmingham City 1
  Winners: Barcelona, 4-1 on aggregate

1961 Birmingham
  Birmingham City 2   Roma 2
Rome
  Roma 2   Birmingham City 0
  Winners: Roma, 4-2 on aggregate

1962 Valencia
  Valencia 6   Barcelona 2
Barcelona
  Barcelona 1   Valencia 1
  Winners: Valencia, 7-3 on aggregate

1963 Zagreb
  Dinamo Zagreb 1   Valencia 2
Valencia
  Valencia 2   Dinamo Zagreb 0
  Winners: Valencia, 4-1 on aggregate

1964 Barcelona
  Real Zaragoza 2   Valencia 1

1965 Turin
  Ferencvaros 1   Juventus 0

1966 Barcelona
  Barcelona 0   Real Zaragoza 1
Zaragoza
  Real Zaragoza 2   Barcelona 4
  Winners: Barcelona, 4-3 on aggregate

1967 Zagreb
  Dinamo Zagreb 2   Leeds United 0
Leeds
  Leeds United 0   Dinamo Zagreb 0
  Winners: Dinamo Zagreb, 2-0 on aggregate

SAY IT AGAIN
DAVID COLEMAN

"Nottingham Forest are having a bad run... they've lost six matches now without winning."

WELL OF COURSE THEY HAVE, OTHERWISE THEY WOULDN'T HAVE LOST!

1968 Leeds
  Leeds United 1   Ferencvaros 0
Budapest
  Ferencvaros 0   Leeds United 0
  Winners: Leeds United, 1-0 on aggregate

1969 Newcastle
  Newcastle United 3   Ujpest Dozsa 0
Budapest
  Ujpest Dozsa 2   Newcastle United 3
  Winners: Newcastle United, 6-2 on aggregate

THE ANORAK SECTION

1970 Brussels
  Anderlecht 3   Arsenal 1
London
  Arsenal 3   Anderlecht 0
  Winners: Arsenal, 4-3 on aggregate

1971 Turin
  Juventus 2   Leeds United 2
Leeds
  Leeds United 1   Juventus 1
  Winners: Leeds United on away goals rule

UEFA CUP FINALS

1972 Wolverhampton
  Wolverhampton W 1   Tottenham H 2
London
  Tottenham H 1   Wolverhampton W 1
  Winners: Tottenham Hotspur, 3-2 on aggregate

1973 Liverpool
  Liverpool 3
          Borrussia Monchengladbach 0
Monchengladbach
  Borrussia Monchengladbach 2
                        Liverpool 0
  Winners: Liverpool, 3-2 on aggregate

1974 London
  Tottenham H 2   Feyenoord 2
Rotterdam
  Feyenoord 2   Tottenham H 0
  Winners: Feyenoord, 4-2 on aggregate

1975 Dusseldorf
  Borrussia Monchengladbach 0
              Twente Eschede 0
Enschende
  Twente Enschende 1
          Borrussia Monchengladbach 5
  Winners: Borrussia Monchengladbach, 5-1 on aggregate

1976 Liverpool
  Liverpool 3   Club Bruge 2
Bruges
  Club Bruge 1   Liverpool 1
  Winners: Liverpool, 4-3 on aggregate

1977 Turin
  Juventus 1   Athletic Bilbao 0
Bilbao
  Athletic Bilbao 2   Juventus 1
  Winners: Juventus on away goals rule

1978 Corsica
  Bastia 0   PSV Eindhoven 0
Eindhoven
  PSV Eindhoven 3   Bastia 0
  Winners: PsV Eindhoven, 3-0 on aggregate

1979 Belgrade
  Red Star Belgrade 1
          Borrussia Monchengladbach 1
Dusseldorf
  Borrussia Monchengladbach 1
                  Red Star Belgrade 0
  Winners: Borrussia Monchengladbach, 2-1 on aggregate

1980 Monchengladbach
  Borrussia Monchengladbach 3
                  Eintracht Frankfurt 2
Frankfurt
  Eintracht Frankfurt 1
          Borrussia Monchengladbach 0
  Winners: Eintracht Frankfurt on away goals rule

1981 Ipswich
  Ipswich Town 3   AZ 67 Alkmaar 0
Amsterdam
  Az 67 Alkmaar 4   Ipswich Town 2
  Winners: Ipswich Town, 5-4 on aggregate

1982 Gothenburg
  IFK Gothenburg 1   Hamburg SV 0
Hamburg
  Hamburg SV 0   IFK Gothenburg 3
  Winners: IFK Gothenburg, 4-0 on aggregate

Action Replays

1983 Brussels
 Anderlecht 1   Benfica 0
Lisbon
 Benfica 1   Anderlecht 1
 Winners: Anderlecht, 2-1 on aggregate

1984 Brussels
 Anderlecht 1   Tottenham H 1
London
 Tottenham H 1   Anderlecht 1 (AET)
 Winners: Tottenham won 4-3 on penalties

1985 Szekesfehervar
 Videoton 0   Real Madrid 3
Madrid
 Real Madrid 0   Videoton 1
 Winners: Real Madrid, 3-1 on aggregate

1986 Madrid
 Real Madrid 5   Koln 1
Berlin
 Koln 2   Real Madrid 0
 Winners: Real Madrid, 5-3 on aggregate

1987 Gothenburg
 IFK Gothenburg 1   Dundee United 0
Dundee
 Dundee United 1   IFK Gothenburg 1
 Winners: IFK Gothenburg, 2-1 on aggregate

1988 Barcelona
 Espanol 3   Bayer Leverkusen 0
Leverkusen
 Bayer Leverkusen 3   Espanol 0 (AET)
 Winners: Bayer Leverkusen won 3-2 on penalties

1989 Naples
 Napoli 2   Stuttgart 1
Stuttgart
 Stuttgart 3   Napoli 3
 Winners: Napoli, 5-4 on aggregate

1990 Turin
 Juventus 3   Fiorentina 1
Florence
 Fiorentina 0   Juventus 0
 Winners: Juventus, 3-1 on aggregate

1991 Milan
 Internazionale 2   Roma 0
Rome
 Roma 1   Internazionale 0
 Winners: Internazionale, 2-1 on aggregate

1992 Turin
 Torino 2   Ajax Amsterdam 2
Amsterdam
 Ajax Amsterdam 0   Torino 0
 Winners: Ajax on away goals rule

1993 Dortmund
 Borussia Dortmund 1   Juventus 3
Turin
 Juventus 3   Borussia Dortmund 0
 Winners: Juventus, 6-1 on aggregate

1994 Vienna
 Salzburg 0   Internazionale 1
Milan
 Internazionale 1   Salzburg 0
 Winners: Internazionale, 2-0 on aggregate

1995 Parma
 Parma 1   Juventus 0
Turin
 Juventus 1   Parma 1
 Winners: Parma, 2-1 on aggregate

1996 Munich
 Bayern Munich 2   Bordeaux 0
Bordeaux
 Bordeaux 1   Bayern Munich 3
 Winners, Bayern Munich 5-1 on aggregate

THE ANORAK SECTION

SAY IT AGAIN

JIM ROSENTHAL:
"So what's an American doing playing in goal for Millwall?"

KASEY KELLER (AMERICAN GOALIE):
"I'm trying to keep the ball out."

NICE ONE, KASEY!

EUROPEAN SUPER CUP

This cup is played annually between the winners of the European Champion's Cup and the European Cup-Winners Cup.

1972 Ajax Amsterdam
 beat Rangers 3-1, 3-2
1973 Ajax Amsterdam
 beat AC Milan 0-1, 6-0
1974 Not contested
1975 Dinamo Kiev beat
 Bayern Munich 1-0, 2-0
1976 Anderlecht
 beat Bayern Munich 4-1, 1-2
1977 Liverpool beat
 Hamburg 1-1, 6-0
1978 Anderlecht beat
 Liverpool 3-1, 1-2
1979 Nottingham Forest
 beat Barcelona 1-0, 1-1
1980 Valencia beat
 Nottingham Forest 1-0, 1-2
1981 Not contested
1982 Aston Villa
 beat Barcelona 0-1, 3-0
1983 Aberdeen
 beat Hamburg 0-0, 2-0
1984 Juventus
 beat Liverpool 2-0
1985 Juventus v Everton not played due to UEFA ban on English clubs
1986 Steaua Bucharest
 beat Dinamo Kiev 1-0
1987 FC Porto beat
 Ajax Amsterdam 1-0, 1-0
1988 KV Mechelen beat
 PSV Eindhoven 3-0, 0-1
1989 AC Milan
 beat Barcelona 1-1, 1-0
1990 Milan
 beat Sampdoria 1-1, 2-0
1991 Man. Utd
 beat Red Star Belgrade 1-0
1992 Barcelona beat
 Werder Bremen 1-1, 2-1
1993 Parma
 beat AC Milan 0-1, 2-0
 (Milan replaced Marseille)
1994 AC Milan beat
 Arsenal 0-0, 2-0
1995 Ajax beat
 Real Zaragoza 1-1, 4-0

WORLD CLUB CUP

This is an annual match played between the champions of Europe and the Champions of South America. From 1960 to 1979 the World Club Cup was decided on points, not goal difference. From 1980 onwards it has been decided by a single match played in Tokyo.

1960 Montevideo
 Penarol 0   Real Madrid 0
Madrid
 Real Madrid 5 Penarol 1

111

Action Replays

1961 Lisbon
    Benfica 1   Penarol 0
Montevideo
    Penarol 5   Benfica 0
Montevideo (play-off)
    Penarol 2   Benfica 1

1962 Rio de Janeiro
    Santos 3   Benfica 2
Lisbon
    Benfica 2   Santos 5

1963 Milan
    Milan 4   Santos 2
Rio de Janeiro
    Santos 4   Milan 2
Rio de Janeiro (play-off)
    Santos 1   Milan 0

1964 Avellanade
    Independiente 1   Internazionale 0
Milan
    Internazionale 2   Independiente 1
Milan (play-off)
    Internazionale 1   Independiente 0 (AET)

1965 Milan
    Internazionale 3   Independiente 0
Avellanada
    Independiente 0   Internazionale 0

1966 Montevideo
    Penarol 2   Real Madrid 0
Madrid
    Real Madrid 0   Penarol 2

1967 Glasgow
    Celtic 1   Racing Club 0
Avellanada
    Racing Club 2   Celtic 1

Montevideo (play-off)
    Racing Club 1   Celtic 0

1968 Buenos Aires
    Estudiantes 1   Man Utd 0
Manchester
    Man. Utd 1   Estudiantes 1

1969 Milan
    Milan 3   Estudiantes 0
Buenos Aires
    Estudiantes 2   Milan 1
Milan won 4-2 on aggregate

1970 Buenos Aires
    Estudiantes 2   Feyenoord 2
Rotterdam:
    Feyenoord 1   Estudiantes 0
Feyenoord won 3-2 on aggregate

1971 Athens
    Panathinaikos 1   Nacional (Uruguay) 1
Montevideo
    Nacional 2   Panathinaikos 1
Nacional won 3-2 on aggregate

1972 Avellanada
    Independiente 1   Ajax Amsterdam 1
Amsterdam
    Ajax Amsterdam 3   Independiente 0
Ajax won 4-1 on aggregate

1973 Rome (one match only)
    Independiente 1   Juventus 0

1974 Buenos Aires.
    Independiente 1   Atletico Madrid 0

112

THE ANORAK SECTION

Madrid
    Atletico Madrid 2
                  Independiente 0
    Atletico won 2-1 on aggregate

1975 Not played

1976 Munich
    Bayern Munich 2   Cruzeiro 0
Bello Horizonte
    Cruzeiro 0   Bayern Munich 0
    Bayern won 2-0 on aggregate

1977 Buenos Aires
    Boca Juniors 2
        Borussia Monchengladbach 2
Karlsruhe
    Borussia Monchengladbach 0
    Boca Juniors 3
    Boca Juniors won 5-2 on aggregate

1978 Not played

1979 Malmo
    Malmo 0   Olimpia 1
Asuncion
    Olimpia 2   Malmo 1
    Olimpia won 3-1 on aggregate

1980 Tokyo
    Nacional Uruguay 1
        Nottingham Forest 0

1981 Tokyo
    Flamengo 3   Liverpool 0

1982 Tokyo
    Penarol 2   Aston Villa 0

1983 Tokyo
    Gremio 2   Hamburg SV 1

1984 Tokyo
    Independiente 1   Liverpool 0

1985 Tokyo
    Juventus 2
        Argentinos Juniors 2 (AET)
    Juventus won 4-2 on penalties

1986 Tokyo
    River Plate 1
        Steaua Bucharest 0

1987 Tokyo
    FC Porto 2   Penarol 1

1988 Tokyo
    Nacional Uruguay 2
        PSV Eindhoven 2 (AET)
    Nacional won 7-6 on penalties

1989 Tokyo
    AC Milan 1
        Nacional Colombia 0 (AET)

1990 Tokyo
    AC Milan 3   Olimpia 0

1991 Tokyo
    Red Star Belgrade 3   Colo Colo. 0

1992 Tokyo
    Sao Paulo 2   Barcelona 1

1993 Tokyo:
    Sao Paulo 3   AC Milan 2

1994 Tokyo
    Velez Sarsfield 2   AC Milan 0

COPA LIBERTADORES (SOUTH AMERICAN CLUB CUP)

The Copa Libertadores is the South American equivalent of the European Cup played for by the champions of South American countries.

Action Replays

1960 Montevideo
   Penarol 1   Olimpia 0
Asuncion
   Olimpia 1   Penarol 1

1961 Montevideo
   Penarol 1   Palmeiras 0
Sao Paulo
   Palmeiras 1   Penarol 1

1962 Montevideo
   Penarol 1   Santos 2
Santos
   Santos 2   Penarol 3
Buenos Aires (Play-off)
   Santos 3   Penarol 0

1963 Rio do Janeiro
   Santos 3   Boca Juniors 2
Buenos Aires
   Boca Juniors 1   Santos 2

1964 Montevideo
   Nacional 0   Independiente 0
Avellaneda
   Independiente 1   Nacional 0

1965 Avellaneda
   Independiente 1   Penarol 0
Montevideo
   Penarol 3   Independiente 1
Santiago (Play-off)
   Independiente 4   Penarol 1

1966 Montevideo
   Penarol 2   River Plate 0
Buenos Aires
   River Plate 3   Penarol 2
Santiago (Play-off)
   Penarol 4   River Plate 2

1967 Avellaneda
   Racing Club 0   Nacional 0
Montevideo
   Nacional 0   Racing Club 0
Santiago (Play-off)
   Racing Club 2   Nacional 1

1968 La Plata
   Estudiantes 2   Palmeiras 1
Sao Paulo
   Palmeiras 3   Esudiantes 1
Montevideo (Play-off)
   Estudiantes 2   Palmeiras 0

1969 Montevideo
   Nacional 0   Estudiantes 1
La Plata
   Estudiantes 2   Nacional 0

1970 La Plata
   Estudiantes 1   Penarol 0
Montevideo
   Penarol 0   Estudiantes 0

1971 La Plata
   Estudiantes 1   Nacional 0
Montevideo
   Nacional 1   Estudiantes 0
Lima (Play-off)
   Nacional 2   Estudiantes 0

1972 Lima
   Universitario 0   Independiente 0
Avellaneda
   Independiente 2   Universitario 1

1973 Avellaneda
   Independiente 1   Colo Colo 1
Santiago
   Colo Colo 0   Independiente 0
Montevideo (Play-off)
   Independiente 2   Colo Colo 1

THE ANORAK SECTION

1974 Sao Paulo
    Sao Paulo 2   Independiente 1
Avellaneda
    Independiente 2   Sao Paulo 0
Santiago (Play-off)
    Independiente 1   Sao Paulo 0

1975 Santiago
    Union Espanola 1
                   Independiente 0
Avellaneda
    Independiente 3
                   Union Espanola 1
Asuncion (Play-off)
    Independiente 2
                   Union Espanola 0

SAY IT AGAIN
BOBBY FERGUSON

"Players win games and players lose games - it's all about players really."

BRILLIANT INSIGHT!

1976 Belo Horizonte
    Cruzeiro 4   River Plate 1
Buenos Aires
    River Plate 2   Cruzeiro 1
Santiago (Play-off)
    Cruzeiro 3   River Plate 2

1977 Buenos Aires
    Boca Juniors 1   Cruzeiro 0
Belo Horizonte
    Cruzeiro 1   Boca Juniors 0
Montevideo
    Boca Juniors 0   Cruzeiro 0

1978 Cali
    Deprotivo Cali 0 Boca Juniors 0
Buenos Aires
    Boca Juniors 4 Deportivo Cali 0

1979 Asuncion
    Olimpia 2   Boca Juniors 0
Buenos Aires
    Boca Juniors 0   Olimpia 0

1980 Porto Alegre
    Internacional PA 0   Nacional 0
Montevideo
    Nacional 1   Internacional PA 0

1981 Rio do Janciro
    Flamengo 2   Cobreloa 1
Santiago
    Cobreloa 1   Flamengo 0
Montevideo (Play-off)
    Flamengo 2   Cobreloa 0

1982 Montevideo
    Penarol 0   Cobreloa 0
Santiago
    Cobreloa 0   Penarol 1

1983 Montevideo
    Penarol 1   Gremio 1
Porto Alegre
    Gremio 2   Penarol 1

1984 Porto Alegre
    Gremio 0   Independiente 1
Avellanda
    Independiente 0   Gremio 0

1985 Buenos Aires
    Argentinos Juniors 1
                   America Cali 0
Cali
    America Cali 1
                   Argentinos Juniors 0
Asuncion (Play-off)
    Argentinos Juniors 1
                   America Cali 1
Argentinos Juniors won 5-4 on penalties

Action Replays

1986 Cali
    America Cali 1   River Plate 2

Buenos Aires
    River Plate 1   America Cali 1

1987 Cali
    America Cali 2   Penarol 0
Montevideo
    Penarol 2   America Cali 1
Santiago (play-off)
    Penarol 1   America Cali 0

1988 Rosario
    Newell's Old Boys 1
        Nacional 0
Montevideo
    Nacional 3
        Newell's Old Boys 0

1989 Asuncion
    Olimpia 2
        Atletico Nacional 0
Bogota
    Atletico Nacional 2,
        Olimpia 0
(Atletico Nacional won 5-4 on penalties)

1990 Asuncion
    Olimpia 2,   Barcelona Ecuador 0
Guayaquil
    Barcelona 1   Olimpia 1

1991 Asuncion
    Olimpia 1   Colo Colo 0
Santiago
    Colo Colo 3   Olimpia 0

1992 Rosario
    Newell's Old Boys 1
        Sao Paulo 0
Sao Paulo
    Sao Paulo 1
        Newell's Old Boys 0
Sao Paulo won 3-2 on penalties

1993 Sao Paulo
    Sao Paulo 5
        Universidad Catolica 1
Santiago
    Universidad Catolica 2
        Sao Paulo 0
Sao Paulo won 5-3 on aggregate

1994 Buenos Aires
    Velez Sarsfield 1,   Sao Paulo 0
Sao Paulo
    Sao Paulo 1,   Velez Sarsfield 0
Velea Sarsfied won 5-3 on penalties

1995 Porto Alegre
    Gremio 3
    Atletico Nationale 1
Colombia
    Atletico Nationale 1   Gremio 1

SOUTH AMERICAN SUPER CUP (TROFEO HAVALANGE)

This is a competition played between previous winners of the Copa Libertadores

Winners
1988 Racing Club
1989 Boca Juniors
1990 Olimpia
1991 Cruzeiro
1992 Cruzeiro
1993 Botafogo
1994 Independiente

CONACAF CHAMPIONS CUP (THE AMERICAN AIRLINES CUP)

This is the top club competition for teams from central America and the Caribbean.

116

THE ANORAK SECTION

Winners
1962 Guadalajara CD (Mexico)
1963 Racing Club (Haiti)
1964 Not completed.
1965 Not completed.
1968 Toluca (Mexico)
1969 Cruz Azul (Mexico)
1970 Cruz Azul (North) Deportivo Saprissa (Central) Transvaal (Caribbean)
1971 Cruz Azul (Mexico)
1972 Olimpia (Honduras)
1973 Transvaal (Surinam)
1974 Municipal (Guatemala)
1975 Atletico Espanol (Mexico)
1976 Aguila (El Salvador)
1977 America (Mexico)
1978 Univ Guadalajara (North) Comunicaciones (Central) Defence Force (Carib.).

SAY IT AGAIN

HOWARD WILKINSON

"I am a firm believer that if you score on goal the other team have to score two to win."

AND IF YOU SCORE TWO, THEY HAVE TO SCORE THREE AND IF YOU SCORE THREE THEY HAVE TO SCORE FOUR........... ETC ETC

1979 Deportivo FAS (El Salvador)
1980 UNAM (Mexico)
1981 Transvaal (Surinam)
1982 UNAM (Mexico)
1983 Atlante (Mexico)
1984 Violette (Haiti)
1985 Defence Force (Trinidad and Tobago)
1986 LD Alajuelense (Costa Rica)
1987 America (Mexico)
1988 Olimpia (Honduras)
1989 UNAM (Mexico)
1990 America (Mexico)
1991 Puebla (Mexico)
1992 America (Mexico)
1993 Deportivo Saprissa (Costa Rica)
1994 Cartagines (Costa Rica)

INTER-AMERICAN CUP

This is a competition between the club champions of South America and CONCACAF. It is played over two legs.

Winners
1968 Estudiantes (Argentina)
1971 Nacional (Uruguay)
1972 Independiente (Argentina)
1974 Independiente (Argentina)
1976 Independiente (Argentina)
1977 America (Mexico)
1979 Olimpia (Paraguay)
1980 UNAM (Mexico)
1985 Argentina Juniors (Argentina)
1986 River Plate (Argentina)
1988 Nacional (Uruguay)
1989 Atletico Nacional (Colombia)
1990 America (Mexico)

AFRICAN CHAMPIONS CUP

This is the African equivalent to the European cup. It is held every year with the champions of each country plus the holders of the cup playing matches on a home and away knock-out basis.

Winners
1964 Oryx Douala (Cameroon)
1965 Not held

Action Replays

1966 Stade Abidjan (Ivory Coast)
1967 TP Englebert (Zaire)
1968 TP Englebert (Zaire)
1969 Al Ismaili (Egypt)
1970 Asante Kotoko (Ghana)
1971 Canon Yaounde (Cameroon)
1972 Hafia Conakry (Ghana)
1973 AS Vita Kinshasa (Zaire)
1974 CARA Brazaville (Congo)
1975 Hafia Conakry (Ghana)
1976 McAlgiers (Algeria)
1977 Hafia Conakry (Ghana)
1978 Canon Yaounde (Cameroon)
1979 Union Douala (Cameroon)
1980 Canon Yaounde (Cameroon)
1981 JE Tizi-Ouzou (Algeria)
1982 Al Ahly (Egypt)
1983 Asant Kotoko (Ghana)
1984 Zamalek (Egypt)
1985 FAR Rabat (Morocco)
1986 Zamalek (Egypt)
1987 Al Ahly (Egypt)
1988 EP Setif (Algeria)
1989 Raja Casablanca (Morocco)
1990 JS Kabylie (Algeria)
1991 Club Africain (Tunisia)
1992 Wydad Casablanca (Morocco)
1993 Zamalek (Egypt)
1994 Esperance (Tunisia)

SAY IT AGAIN

DICKIE DAVIES:

"What's he going to be telling his team at half-time, Denis?"

DENIS LAW:

"He'll be telling them that there are 45 minutes left to play..."

1982 Al Mokaoulum (Egypt)
1983 Al Mokaoulum (Egypt)
1984 Al Ahly (Egypt)
1985 Al Ahly (Egypt)
1986 Al Ahly (Egypt)
1987 Gor Mahia (Kenya)
1988 CA Bizerte (Tunisia)
1989 Al Merreikh (Sudan)
1990 BCC Lions (Nigeria)
1991 Power Dynamos (Zambia)
1992 Africa Sports (Ivory Coast)
1993 Al Ahly (Egypt)
1994 Daring Club (Zaire)

AFRICAN CUP-WINNERS CUP
Africa's premier competition for the winners of the continent's knock-out challenge cups.

Winners
1975 Tonnerre Younde (Cameroon)
1976 Shooting Stars (Nigeria)
1977 Enugu Rangers (Nigeria)
1978 Horoya Conakry (Guinea)
1979 Canon Yaounde (Cameron)
1980 TP Mazembe (Zaire)
1981 Union Douala (Cameroon)

CAF CUP
This recent competition is Africa's equivalent to the UEFA Cup.

Winners
1992 Shooting Stars (Nigeria)
1993 Stella Abidjan Ivory Coast)
1994 Bendel Insurance (Nigeria)

THE ANORAK SECTION

ENGLISH FOOTBALL LEAGUE

Season Champions Pts Runners-up Pts

1888-89 Preston NE 40 Aston Villa 29
1889-90 Preston NE 33 Everton 31
1890-91 Everton 29 Preston NE 27
1891-92 Sunderland 42 Preston NE 37

FIRST DIVISION
1892-93 Sunderland 48 Preston NE 37
1893-94 Aston Villa 44 Sunderland 38
1894-95 Sunderland 47 Everton 42
1895-96 Aston Villa 45 Derby County 41
1896-97 Aston Villa 47 Sheffield Utd 36
1897-98 Sheffield Utd 42 Sunderland 37
1898-99 Aston Villa 45 Liverpool 43
1899-1900 Aston Villa 50 Sheffield Utd 48
1900-01 Liverpool 45 Sunderland 43
1901-02 Sunderland 44 Everton 41
1902-03 Sheffield Wed 42 Aston Villa 41
1903-04 Sheffield Wed 47 Manchester C 44
1904-05 Newcastle Utd 48 Everton 47
1905-06 Liverpool 51 Preston NE 47
1906-07 Newcastle Utd 51 Bristol City 48
1907-08 Man Utd 52 Aston Villa 43
1908-09 Newcastle Utd 53 Everton 46
1909-10 Aston Villa 53 Liverpool 48
1910-11 Man Utd 52 Aston Villa 51
1911-12 Blackburn R 49 Everton 46
1912-13 Sunderland 54 Aston Villa 50
1913-14 Blackburn R 51 Aston Villa 44
1914-15 Everton 46 Oldham Ath 45

SAY IT AGAIN

MIKE ENGLAND

"Well, as for Ian Rush - he's perfectly fit - apart, that is from his physical fitness..."

1919-20 WBA 60 Burnley 51
1920-21 Burnley 59 Manchester C 54
1921-22 Liverpool 57 Tottenham H 51
1922-23 Liverpool 60 Sunderland 54
1923-24 Huddersfield T 57 Cardiff C 57
1924-25 Huddersfield T 58 WBA 56
1925-26 Huddersfield T 57 Arsenal 52
1926-27 Newcastle Utd 56 Huddersfield T 51
1927-28 Everton 53 Huddersfield T 51
1928-29 Sheffield Wed 52 Leicester C 51
1929-30 Sheffield Wed 60 Derby County 50
1930-31 Arsenal 66 Aston Villa 59
1931-32 Everton 56 Arsenal 54
1932-33 Arsenal 58 Aston Villa 54
1933-34 Arsenal 59 Huddersfield T 56
1934-35 Arsenal 58 Sunderland 54
1935-36 Sunderland 56 Derby County 48
1936-37 Manchester C 57 Charlton Ath 54
1937-38 Arsenal 52 Wolves 51
1938-39 Everton 59 Wolves 55
1946-47 Liverpool 57 Man Utd 56
1947-48 Arsenal 59 Man Utd 52
1948-49 Portsmouth 58 Man Utd 53
1949-50 Portsmouth 53 Wolves 53
1950-51 Tottenham H 60 Man Utd 56
1951-52 Man Utd 57 Tottenham H 53
1952-53 Arsenal 54 Preston NE 54
1953-54 Wolves 57 WBA 53
1954-55 Chelsea 52 Wolves 48
1955-56 Man Utd 60 Blackpool 49
1956-57 Man Utd 64 Tottenham H 56
1957-58 Wolves 64 Preston NE 59
1958-59 Wolves 61 Man Utd 55
1959-60 Burnley 55 Wolves 54
1960-61 Tottenham H 66 Sheffield Wed 58
1961-62 Ipswich T 56 Burnley 53
1962-63 Everton 61 Tottenham H 55
1963-64 Liverpool 57 Man Utd 53
1964-65 Man Utd 61 Leeds Utd 61
1965-66 Liverpool 61 Leeds Utd 55
1966-67 Man Utd 60 Nottm Forest 56
1967-68 Manchester C 58 Man Utd 56
1968-69 Leeds Utd 67 Liverpool 61
1969-70 Everton 66 Leeds Utd 57
1970-71 Arsenal 65 Leeds Utd 64

119

Action Replays

1971-72 Derby County	58	Leeds Utd	57
1972-73 Liverpool	60	Arsenal	57
1973-74 Leeds Utd	62	Liverpool	57
1974-75 Derby County	53	Liverpool	51
1975-76 Liverpool	60	QPR	59
1976-77 Liverpool	57	Manchester C	56
1977-78 Nottm Forest	64	Liverpool	57
1978-79 Liverpool	68	Nottm Forest	60
1979-80 Liverpool	60	Man. Utd	58
1980-81 Aston Villa	60	Ipswich T	56
1981-82 Liverpool	87	Ipswich T	83
1982-83 Liverpool	82	Watford	71
1983-84 Liverpool	80	Southampton	77
1984-85 Everton	90	Liverpool	77
1985-86 Liverpool	88	Everton	86
1986-87 Everton	86	Liverpool	77
1987-88 Liverpool	90	Man Utd	81
1988-89 Arsenal	76	Liverpool	76
1989-90 Liverpool	79	Aston Villa	70
1990-91 Arsenal	83	Liverpool	76
1991-92 Leeds Utd	82	Man Utd	78

FA PREMIER LEAGUE

1992-93 Man Utd	84	Aston Villa	74
1993-94 Man Utd	92	Blackburn R	84
1994-95 Blackburn R	89	Man Utd	88
1995-96 Man Utd	82	Newcastle Utd	78

FA CUP

1872 Wanderers 1.....Royal Engineers 0
1873 Wanderers 2 ..Oxford University 0
1874 Oxford University 2............................
...........................Royal Engineers 0
1875 Royal Engineers 1 Old Etonians 1
 Replay 2-0
1876 Wanderers 0 ....Old Etonians 0
 Replay 3-0
1877 Wanderers 2. Oxford University 0
 (AET)
1878 Wanderers 3.......Royal Engineers-
 (AET)
1879 Old Etonians 1 Clapham Rovers 0
1880 Clapham Rovers 1 ..Oxford Uni 0
1881 Old Carthusians 3 Old Etonians 0
1882 Old Etonians 1 ...... Blackburn R 0
1883 Blackburn Olympic 2.....................
..............................Old Etonians 1 (AET)
1884 Blackburn R 2 ....
..........................Queens Park Glasgow 1
1885 Blackburn R 2 ....
..........................Queens Park Glasgow 0
1886 Blackburn R 0 .... WBA 0
 Replay 2-0
1887 Aston Villa 2 ....WBA 0
1888 WBA 2 ....Preston NE 1
1889 Preston NE 3...................Wolves 0
1890 Blackburn R 6 .....Sheffield Wed 1
1891 Blackburn R 3 .....Notts County 1
1892 WBA 3...................... Aston Villa 0
1893 Wolves 1 ....Everton 0
1894 Notts County 4 ....Bolton W 1
1895 Aston Villa 1................... WBA 0
1896 Sheffield Wed 2 ....Wolves 1
1897 Aston Villa 3 ....Everton 2
1898 Nottm Forest 3 ...Derby County 1
1899 Sheffield Utd 4 ...Derby County 1
1900 Bury 4 ....Southampton 0
1901 Tottenham H 2..... Sheffield Utd 2
 Replay 3-1
1902 Sheffield Utd 1 ......Southampton 1
 Replay 2-1
1903 Bury 6 ....Derby County 0
1904 Manchester C 1 ....Bolton W 0
1905 Aston Villa 2 .....Newcastle Utd 0
1906 Everton 1 ....Newcastle Utd 0
1907 Sheffield Wed 2 .... Everton 1
1908 Wolves 3 ....Newcastle Utd 1
1909 Man Utd 1 .... Bristol C 0
1910 Newcastle Utd 1 ....Barnsley 1
 Replay 2-0
1911 Bradford C 0 ......Newcastle Utd 0
 Replay 1-0

THE ANORAK SECTION

1912 Barnsley 0 ....WBA 0
Replay 1-0
1913 Aston Villa 1 .... Sunderland 0
1914 Burnley 1 ....Liverpool 0
1915 Sheffield Utd 3 ....Chelsea 0
1920 Aston Villa 1 .....Huddersfield T 0 (AET)
1921 Tottenham H 1 .... Wolves 0
1922 Huddersfield T 1 .... Preston NE 0
1923 Bolton W 2 ....West Ham Utd 0
1924 Newcastle Utd 2 .....Aston Villa 0
1925 Sheffield Utd 1 ....Cardiff C 0
1926 Bolton W 1 ....Manchester C 0
1927 Cardiff C 1 .... Arsenal 0
1928 Blackburn R 3... Huddersfield T 1
1929 Bolton W 2 ,,,,,,,, Portsmouth 0
1930 Arsenal 2 ....Huddersfield T 0
1931 WBA 2 ....Birmingham C 1
1932 Newcastle Utd 2 ....Arsenal 1
1933 Everton 3 ....Manchester C 0
1934 Manchester C 2 ..... Portsmouth 1
1935 Sheffield Wed 4 ....WBA 2
1936 Arsenal 1 .... Sheffield Utd 0
1937 Sunderland 3 ....Preston NE 1
1938 Preston NE 1 .... Huddersfield 0 (AET)
1939 Portsmouth 4 .... Wolves 1
1946 Derby County 4 ...Charlton Ath 1 (AET)
1947 Charlton Ath 1 ....Burnley 0 (AET)
1948 Man Utd 4 ....Blackpool 2
1949 Wolves 3 ....Leicester C 1
1950 Arsenal 2 .... Liverpool 0
1951 Newcastle Utd 2 ....Blackpool 0
1952 Newcastle Utd 1 ....Arsenal 0
1953 Blackpool 4 ....Bolton W 3
1954 WBA 3 ....Preston NE 2
1955 Newcastle Utd 3 .Manchester C 1

1956 Manchester C 3 . Birmingham C 1
1957 Aston Villa 2 ....Man Utd 1
1958 Bolton W 2 ....Man Utd 0
1959 Nottm Forest 2 ....Luton T 1
1960 Wolves 3 .... Blackburn R 0
1961 Tottenham H 2 .... Leicester C 0
1962 Tottenham H 3 ....Burnley 1
1963 Man Utd 3 ....Leicester C 1
1964 West Ham Utd 3 ....Preston NE 2
1965 Liverpool 2 ....Leeds Utd 1 (AET)
1966 Everton 3 ....Sheffield Wed 2
1967 Tottenham H 2 .... Chelsea 1
1968 WBA 1 ....Everton 0 (AET)
1969 Manchester C 1 ......Leicester C 0
1970 Chelsea 2 ....Leeds Utd 2
Replay 2-1
1971 Arsenal 2 ,,,,,,,,,,,..........Liverpool 1
1972 Leeds Utd 1 .... Arsenal 0
1973 Sunderland 1 ....Leeds Utd 0
1974 Liverpool 3 ....Newcastle Utd 0
1975 West Ham Utd 2 ....Fulham 0
1976 Southampton 1 ....Man Utd 0
1977 Man Utd 2 ....Liverpool 1
1978 Ipswich T 1 .... Arsenal 0
1979 Arsenal 3 ....Man Utd 2
1980 West Ham Utd 1 ....Arsenal 0
1981 Tottenham H 1... Manchester C 1
Replay 3-2
1982 Tottenham H 1 ....QPR 1
Replay 1-0
1983 Manchester U 2 Brighton H A 2
Replay 4-0
1984 Everton 2 ....Watford 0
1985 Man Utd 1 ....Everton 0
1986 Liverpool 3 ....Everton 1
1987 Coventry C 3 ....Tottenham H 2
1988 Wimbledon 1 .... Liverpool 0
1989 Liverpool 3 ....Everton 2 (AET)

121

Action Replays

1990 Man Utd 3............Crystal Palace 3
 Replay 1-0
1991 Tottenham H 2 ....Nottm Forest 1
 (AET)
1992 Liverpool 2 .... Sunderland 0
1993 Arsenal 1 ....Sheffield Wed 1
 Replay 2 - 1
1994 Man Utd 4 ....Chelsea 0
1995 Everton 1 ....Man Utd 0
1996 Man Utd 1 ....Liverpool 0

FOOTBALL LEAGUE CUP

1961 Aston Villa............Rotherham Utd
 0-2, 3-0 (AET)
1962 Norwich C ....Rochdale
 3-0, 1-0
1963 Birmingham C.............Aston Villa
 3-1, 0-0
1964 Leicester C ....Stoke C
 1-1, 3-2
1965 Chelsea.........................Leicester C
 3-2, 0-0
1966 WBA........................West Ham Utd
 1-2, 4-1
One leg final introduced
1967 QPR 3.....................................WBA 2
1968 Leeds Utd 1 .... Arsenal 0
1969 Swindon T 3.................... Arsenal 1
1970 Manchester C 2 .... WBA 1
1971 Tottenham H 2 ....Aston Villa 0
1972 Stoke C 2 ....Chelsea 1
1973 Tottenham H 1 ....Norwich C 0
1974 Wolves 2 .... Manchester C 1
1975 Aston Villa 1 ....Norwich C 0

1976 Manchester C 2 .Newcastle Utd 1
1977 Aston Villa 0 ....Everton 0 (AET)
 Replay 1-1 (AET) 3-2
1978 Nottm Forest 0 ....Liverpool 0
 (AET) 1-0
1979 Nottm Forest 3 ....Southampton 2
1980 Wolves 1...............Nottm Forest 0
1981 Liverpool 2 ....West Ham Utd 1
 (AET)

FOOTBALL LEAGUE MILK CUP
1982 Liverpool 3 .Tottenham H 1 (AET)
1983 Liverpool 2 ....Man Utd 1 (AET)
1984 Liverpool 0 ....Everton 0
 Replay 1-0
1985 Norwich C 1 ....Sunderland-0
1986 Oxford Utd 3 ....QPR 0

SAY IT AGAIN
BOBBY ROBSON

"Well, we got nine and you can't score more than that."

TEN? ELEVEN? TWELVE?....ETC ETC

FOOTBALL LEAGUE LITTLEWOODS CUP

1987 Arsenal 2   Liverpool 1
1988 Luton Town 3   Arsenal 2
1989 Nottm Forest 3   Luton Town 1
1990 Nottm Forest 1   Oldham Ath 0

THE ANORAK SECTION

RUMBELOWS LEAGUE CUP

1991 Sheffield Wed 1 . . . . . Man Utd 0
1992 Man Utd 1 . . . . . Nottm Forest 0

COCA-COLA CUP

1993 Arsenal 1 . . . . . . Sheffield Wed 1
1994 Aston Villa 3 . . . . Man Utd 1
1995 Liverpool 2 . Bolton Wanderers 1
1996 Aston Villa 3 . . . . . . Leeds Utd 0

SCOTTISH FIRST DIVISION

Season Champions Pts   Runners-up Pts

1890-91 Dumbarton 29 . . . Rangers 29
1891-92 Dumbarton 37 . . . Celtic 35
1892-93 Celtic 29 . . . . Rangers 28
1893-94 Celtic 29 . . . . Hearts 26
1894-95 Hearts 31 . . . . Celtic 26
1895-96 Celtic 30 . . . . Rangers 26
1896-97 Hearts 28 . . . . . Hibernian 26
1897-98 Celtic 33 . . . . Rangers 29
1898-99 Rangers 36 . . . . Hearts 26
1899-1900 Rangers 32 . . . . . . Celtic 25
1900-01 Rangers 35 . . . . Celtic 29
1901-02 Rangers 28 . . . . Celtic 26
1902-03 Hibernian 37 . . . . . Dundee 31
1903-04 Third Lanark 43 . . Hearts 39
1904-05 Celtic 41 . . . . Rangers 41
1905-06 Celtic 49 . . . . Hearts 43
1906-07 Celtic 55 . . . . Dundee 48
1907-08 Celtic 55 . . . . Falkirk 51
1908-09 Celtic 51 . . . . . . Dundee 50
1909-10 Celtic 54 . . . . Falkirk 52
1910-11 Rangers 52 . . . . . Aberdeen 48
1911-12 Rangers 51 . . . . Celtic 45
1912-13 Rangers 53 . . . . Celtic 49
1913-14 Celtic 65 . . . . Rangers 59
1914-15 Celtic 65 . . . . Hearts 61
1915-16 Celtic 67 . . . . Rangers 56
1916-17 Celtic 64 . . . . Morton 54
1917-18 Rangers 56 . . . . Celtic 55

1918-19 Celtic 58 . . . . Rangers 57
1919-20 Rangers 71 . . . . Celtic 68
1920-21 Rangers 76 . . . . Celtic 66
1921-22 Celtic 67 . . . . Rangers 66
1922-23 Rangers 55 . Airdrieonians 50
1923-24 Rangers 59 . Airdrieonians 50
1924-25 Rangers 60 . Airdrieonians 57
1925-26 Celtic 58 . . . Airdrieonians 50
1926-27 Rangers 56 . . . Motherwell 51
1927-28 Rangers 60 . . . . Celtic 55
1928-29 Rangers 67 . . . . Celtic 51
1929-30 Rangers 60 . . . Motherwell 55
1930-31 Rangers 60 . . . . Celtic 58
1931-32 Motherwell 66 . . . Rangers 61
1932-33 Rangers 62 . . . Motherwell 59
1933-34 Rangers 66 . . . Motherwell 62
1934-35 Rangers 55 . . . . Celtic 52
1935-36 Celtic 66 . . . . Rangers 61
1936-37 Rangers 61 . . . . . Aberdeen 54
1937-38 Celtic 61 . . . . Hearts 58
1938-39 Rangers 59 . . . . Celtic 48
1946-47 Rangers 46 . . . . Hibernian 44
1947-48 Hibernian 48 . . . . Rangers 46
1948-49 Rangers 46 . . . . . . Dundee 45
1949-50 Rangers 50 . . . . Hibernian 49
1950-51 Hibernian 48 . . . . Rangers 38
1951-52 Hibernian 45 . . . . Rangers 41
1952-53 Rangers 43 . . . . Hibernian 43
1953-54 Celtic 43 . . . . Hearts 38
1954-55 Aberdeen 49 . . . . Celtic 46
1955-56 Rangers 52 . . . . . Aberdeen 46
1956-57 Rangers 55 . . . . Hearts 53
1957-58 Hearts 62 . . . . Rangers 49
1958-59 Rangers 50 . . . . Hearts 48
1959-60 Hearts 54 . . . . . Kilmarnock 50
1960-61 Rangers 51 . . . Kilmarnock 50
1961-62 Dundee 54 . . . . . . Rangers 51
1962-63 Rangers 57 . . . Kilmarnock 48
1963-64 Rangers 55 . . . Kilmarnock 49
1964-65 Kilmarnock 50 . . . . Hearts 50
1965-66 Celtic 57 . . . . Rangers 55
1966-67 Celtic 58 . . . . Rangers 55
1967-68 Celtic 63 . . . . Rangers 61
1968-69 Celtic 54 . . . . Rangers 49
1969-70 Celtic 57 . . . . Rangers 45

123

Action Replays

1970-71 Celtic 56 ...... Aberdeen 54
1971-72 Celtic 60 .... Aberdeen 50
1972-73 Celtic 57 .... Rangers 56
1973-74 Celtic 53 ...... Hibernian 49
1974-75 Rangers 56 .... Hibernian 49

PREMIER DIVISION
(first division renamed)
1975-76 Rangers 54 .... Celtic 48
1976-77 Celtic 55 .... Rangers 46
1977-78 Rangers 55 ..... Aberdeen 53
1978-79 Celtic 48 .... Rangers 45
1979-80 Aberdeen 48 .... Celtic 47
1980-81 Celtic 56 .... Aberdeen 49
1981-82 Celtic 55 .... Aberdeen 53
1982-83 Dundee Utd 56 .... Celtic- 55
1983-84 Aberdeen 57 .... Celtic 50
1984-85 Aberdeen 59 .... Celtic 52
1971-72 Celtic 60 .... Aberdeen 50
1972-73 Celtic 57 .... Rangers 56
1973-74 Celtic 53 ...... Hibernian 49
1974-75 Rangers 56 .... Hibernian 49

PREMIER DIVISION
(first division renamed)
1975-76 Rangers 54 .... Celtic 48
1976-77 Celtic 55 .... Rangers 46
1977-78 Rangers 55 ..... Aberdeen 53
1978-79 Celtic 48 .... Rangers 45
1979-80 Aberdeen 48 .... Celtic 47
1980-81 Celtic 56 .... Aberdeen 49
1981-82 Celtic 55 .... Aberdeen 53
1982-83 Dundee Utd 56 .... Celtic- 55
1983-84 Aberdeen 57 .... Celtic 50
1984-85 Aberdeen 59 .... Celtic 52
1985-86 Celtic 50 .... Hearts 50
1986-87 Rangers 69 .... Celtic 63
1987-88 Celtic 72 .... Hearts 62
1988-89 Rangers 56 ..... Aberdeen 50
1989-90 Rangers 51 ..... Aberdeen 44
1990-91 Rangers 55 ..... Aberdeen 53
1991-92 Rangers 72 .... Hearts 63
1992-93 Rangers 73 ..... Aberdeen 64
1993-94 Rangers 58 ..... Aberdeen 55
1994-95 Rangers 69 ... Motherwell 54

SAY IT AGAIN

VETERAN GOALKEEPER JOHN BURRIDGE

"People say I'm eccentric but I'm just enthusiastic. I still love the game.

"That's why I take a ball to bed and put on my gloves and boots to watch Match of the Day."

KEEP TAKING THE PILLS....

SCOTTISH FA CUP

1874 Queen's Park 2 ... Clydesdale 0
1875 Queen's Park 3....... Renton 0
1876 Queen's Park 1 . Third Lanark 1,
  Replay 2-0
1877 Vale of Leven 0 ...... Rangers 0
  Replay 1-1
  Replay 3-2
1878 Vale of Leven 1 . Third Lanark 0
1879 Vale of Leven .... Rangers
Rangers failed to turn up for the replay after a 1-1 draw. Vale of Leven awarded Cup
1880 Queen's Park 3 .. Thornlibank -0
1881 Queen's Park 3 ... Dumbarton 1
1882 Queen's Park 2 ... Dumbarton 2
  Replay 4-1
1883 Dumbarton 2 ... Vale of Leven 2
  Replay 2 -1
1884 Queen's Park..... Vale of Leven
Vale of Leven failed to appear for the final. Queen's Park awarded the Cup
1885 Renton 0 ...... Vale of Leven 0
  Replay 3-1

THE ANORAK SECTION

1886 Queen's Park 3 .... Renton 1
1887 Hibernian 2 ...... Dumbarton 1
1888 Renton 6 .... Cambuslang 1
1889 Third Lanark 3 .... Celtic 0
  Replay 2-1
Replay ordered because of playing conditions in the first game
1890 Queen's Park 1 . Vale of Leven 1
  Replay 2-1
1891 Hearts 1 .... Dumbarton 0
1892 Celtic 5 .... Queen's Park 1
After a protested game which Celtic won 1-0
1893 Queen's Park 2 .... Celtic 1
1894 Rangers 3 .... Celtic 1
1895 St Bernard's 2 .... Renton 1
1896 Hearts 3 .... Hibernian 1
1897 Rangers 5 .... Dumbarton 1
1898 Rangers 2 .... Kilmarnock 0
1899 Celtic 2 .... Rangers 0
1900 Celtic 4 .... Queen's Park 3
1901 Hearts 4 .... Celtic 3
1902 Hibernian 1 .... Celtic 0
1903 Rangers 1 .... Hearts 1
  Replay 0-0
  Replay 2-0
1904 Celtic 3 .... Rangers 2
1905 Third Lanark 0 ...... Rangers 0
  Replay 3-1
1906 Hearts 1 ...... Third Lanark 0
1907 Celtic 3 .... Hearts 0
1908 Celtic 5 .... St Mirren 1
1909 Celtic 2 .... Rangers 2
  Replay 1-1
The cup was withheld because of a riot after two drawn games.
1910 Dundee 2 .... Clyde 2
  Replay 0-0
  Replay 2-1
1911 Celtic 0 .... Hamilton A 0
  Replay 2-0
1912 Celtic 2 .... Clyde 0
1913 Falkirk 2 .... Raith R 0
1914 Celtic 0 .... Hibernian 0
  Replay 1-1
1920 Kilmarnock 3 .... Albion R 2

1921 Partick T 1 .... Rangers 0
1922 Morton 1 .... Rangers 0
1923 Celtic 1 .... Hibernian 0
1924 Airdrieonians 2 .... Hibernian 0
1925 Celtic 2 .... Dundee 1
1926 St Mirren 2 .... Celtic 0
1927 Celtic 3 .... East Fife 1
1928 Rangers 4 .... Celtic 0
1929 Kilmarnock 2 ...... Rangers 0
1930 Rangers 0 .... Partick T 0
  Replay 2-1
1931 Celtic 2 .... Motherwell 2
  Replay 4-2
1932 Rangers 1 .... Kilmarnock 1
  Replay 3-0
1933 Celtic 1 .... Motherwell 0
1934 Rangers 5 .... St Mirren 0
1935 Rangers 2 .... Hamilton A 1
1936 Rangers 1 ..... Third Lanark 0
1937 Celtic 2 .... Aberdeen 1
1938 East Fife 1 .... Kilmarnock 1
  Replay 4-2
1939 Clyde 4 .... Motherwell 0
1947 Aberdeen 2 .... Hibernian 1
1948 Rangers 1 .... Morton 1
  Replay 1-0
1949 Rangers 4 .... Clyde 1
1950 Rangers 3 .... East Fife 0
1951 Celtic 1 .... Motherwell 0
1952 Motherwell 4 .... Dundee 0
1953 Rangers 1 .... Aberdeen 1
  Replay 1-0
1954 Celtic 2 .... Aberdeen 1
1955 Clyde 1 Celtic 1
  Replay 1-0
1956 Hearts 3 .... Celtic 1
1957 Falkirk 1 .... Kilmarnock 1
  Replay 2-1
1958 Clyde 1 .... Hibernian 0
1959 St Mirren 3 .... Aberdeen 1
1960 Rangers 2 .... Kilmarnock 0
1961 Dunfermline A 0 .... Celtic 0
  Replay 2-0
1962 Rangers 2 .... St Mirren 0

Action Replays

1963 Rangers 1 . . . . Celtic 1
Replay 3-0
1964 Rangers 3 . . . . Dundee 1
1965 Celtic 3 . . . . Dunfermline A 2
1966 Rangers 0 . . . . Celtic 0
Replay 1-0
1967 Celtic 2 . . . . Aberdeen 0
1968 Dunfermline A 3 . . . . . . Hearts 1
1969 Celtic 4 . . . . Rangers 0
1970 Aberdeen 3 . . . . Celtic 1
1971 Celtic 1 . . . . Rangers 1
Replay 2-1
1972 Celtic 6 . . . . Hibernian 1
1973 Rangers 3 . . . . Celtic 2
1974 Celtic 3 . . . . Dundee Utd 0
1975 Celtic 3 . . . . Airdrieonians 1
1976 Rangers 3 . . . . Hearts 1
1977 Celtic 1 . . . . Rangers 0
1978 Rangers 2 . . . . Aberdeen 1
1979 Rangers 0 . . . . Hibernian 0
Replay 0-0
Replay 3-2
1980 Celtic 1 . . . . Rangers 0
1981 Rangers 0 . . . . . . Dundee Utd 0
Replay 4-1
1982 Aberdeen 4 . . . . Rangers 1
1983 Aberdeen 1 . . . . . Rangers 0 (AET)
1984 Aberdeen 2 . . . . . . Celtic 1 (AET)
1985 Celtic 2 . . . . Dundee Utd 1
1986 Aberdeen 3 . . . . Hearts 0
1987 St Mirren 1 . . . . . . Dundee Utd 0
1988 Celtic 2 . . . . Dundee Utd 1
1989 Celtic 1 . . . . Rangers 0
1990 Aberdeen 0 . . . . Celtic 0
Aberdeen won 9-8 on penalties
1991 Motherwell 4 . . . . Dundee Utd 3
1992 Rangers 2 . . . . . . Airdrieonians 1
1993 Rangers 2 . . . . Aberdeen 1
1994 Dundee Utd 1 . . . . Rangers 0
1995 Celtic 1 . . . . Airdrieonians 0
1996 Rangers 5 . . . . Hearts 1

SCOTTISH LEAGUE CUP

1946-47 Rangers 4 . . . . Aberdeen 0
1947-48 East Fife 0 . . . . Falkirk 0
Replay 4-1
1948-49 Rangers 2 . . . . Raith Rovers 0
1949-50 East Fife 3 Dunfermline Ath 0
1950-51 Motherwell 3 . . . . Hibernian 0
1951-52 Dundee 3 . . . . Rangers 2
1952-53 Dundee 2 . . . . . Kilmarnock 0
1953-54 East Fife 3 . . . . . . Partick T 2
1954-55 Hearts 4 . . . . . . Motherwell 2
1955-56 Aberdeen 2 . . . . . St Mirren 1
1956-57 Celtic 0 . . . . Partick T 0
Replay 3-0
1957-58 Celtic 7 . . . . Rangers 1
1958-59 Hearts 5 . . . . Partick T 1
1959-60 Hearts 2 . . . . Third Lanark 1
1960-61 Rangers 2 . . . . . Kilmarnock 0
1961-62 Rangers 1 . . . . Hearts 1
Replay 3-1
1962-63 Hearts 1 . . . . . . Kilmarnock 0
1963-64 Rangers 5 . . . . Morton 0
1964-65 Rangers 2 . . . . Celtic 1
1965-66 Celtic 2 . . . . Rangers 1
1966-67 Celtic 1 . . . . Rangers 0
1967-68 Celtic 5 . . . . Dundee 3
1968-69 Celtic 6 . . . . Hibernian 2
1969-70 Celtic 1 . . . . . . St Johnstone 0
1970-71 Rangers 1 . . . . Celtic 0
1971-72 Partick T 4 . . . . Celtic 1
1972-73 Hibernian 2 . . . . Celtic 1
1973-74 Dundee 1 . . . . Celtic 0
1974-75 Celtic 6 . . . . Hibernian 3
1975-76 Rangers 1 . . . . Celtic 0
1976-77 Aberdeen 2 . . . . Celtic 1
1977-78 Rangers 2 . . . . Celtic 1
1978-79 Rangers 2 . . . . Aberdeen 1
1979-80 Dundee Utd 0 . . . Aberdeen 0
Replay 3-0
1980-81 Dundee Utd 3 . . . . . Dundee 0
1981-82 Rangers 2 . . . . Dundee Utd 1
1982-83 Celtic 2 . . . . Rangers 1
1983-84 Rangers 3 . . . . Celtic 2
1984-85 Rangers 1 . . . . Dundee Utd 0

THE ANORAK SECTION

1985-86 Aberdeen 3 ..... Hibernian 0
1986-87 Rangers 2 .... Celtic 1
1987-88 Rangers 3 .... Aberdeen 3
Rangers won 5-3 on penalties
1988-89 Rangers 3 .... Aberdeen 2
1989-90 Aberdeen 2 .... Rangers 1
1990-91 Rangers 2 .... Celtic 1
1991-92 Hibernian 2 Dunfermline A 0
1992-93 Rangers 2....... Aberdeen 1
1993-94 Rangers 2 ...... Hibernian 1
1994-95 Raith Rovers 0 ...... Celtic 0
Raith Rovers won 6-5 on penalties
1995-96 Aberdeen 2....... Dundee 0

LEAGUE OF WALES
1993 .... Cwmbran Town
1994 .... Bangor C
1995 .... Bangor C

LEAGUE OF WALES CUP

1993 Caersws   Afan Lido   Penalties
1994 Afan Lido 1 Bangor 0
1995 Llansantffraid 2 Ton Pentre 1

WELSH CUP FINALS

1878 Wrexham 1 .... Druids 0
1879 Newtown 1 .... Wrexham 0
1880 Druids 2 .... Ruthin 1
1881 Druids 2 Newtown White Stars 0
1882 Druids 2 .... Northwich 1
1883 Wrexham 1 .... Druids 0
1884 Oswestry 3 .... Druids 2
1885 Druids 2 .... Oswestry 0
1886 Druids 5 .... Newtown 0
1887 Chirk 4 .... Davenham 2
1888 Chirk 5 .... Newtown 0
1889 Bangor 2 .... Northwich 1
1890 Chirk 1 .... Wrexham 0
1891 Shrewsbury T 5 ... Wrexham 2
1892 Chirk 2 ...... Westminster R 1
1893 Wrexham 2 .... Chirk 1
1894 Chirk 2 ...... Westminster R 0
1895 Newtown 3 ...... Wrexham 2
1896 Bangor 3 .... Wrexham 1
1897 Wrexham 2 .... Newtown 0
1898 Druids 1 .... Wrexham 1
Replay 2-1
1899 Druids 2 .... Wrexham 2
Replay 1-0
1900 Aberystwyth 3 .... Druids 0
1901 Oswestry 1 .... Druids 0
1902 Wellington 1 ..... Wrexham 0
1903 Wrexham 3 ...... Aberaman 0
1904 Druids 3 .... Aberdare 2
1905 Wrexham 3 .... Aberdare 0
1906 Wellington 3 ..... Whitchurch 2
1907 Oswestry 2 .... Whitchurch 0
1908 Chester 3 ..... Connah's Quay 1
1909 Wrexham 1 .... Chester 0
1910 Wrexham 2 .... Chester 1
1911 Wrexham 6 .. Connah's Quay 1
1912 Cardiff C 0 .... Pontypridd 0
Replay 3-0
1913 Swansea 0 .... Pontypridd 0
Replay 1-0
1914 Wrexham 1 .... Llanelly 1
Replay 3-0
1915 Wrexham 0 .... Swansea 0
Replay 1-0
1920 Cardiff C 2 .... Wrexham 1
1921 Wrexham 1 ...... Pontypridd 1
Replay 3-1
1922 Cardiff C 2 ...... Ton Pentre 0
1923 Cardiff C 3 .... Aberdare 2
1924 Wrexham 2 .... Merthyr 2
Replay 1-0
1925 Wrexham 3 .... Flint 1
1926 Ebbw Vale 3 .... Swansea 2
1927 Cardiff C 0 .... Rhyl 0
Replay 4-2
1928 Cardiff C 2 .... Bangor 0
1929 Connah's Quay 3 ... Cardiff C 0
1930 Cardiff C 0 .... Rhyl 0
Replay 4-2
1931 Wrexham 7 ..... Shrewsbury 0
1932 Swansea 1 .... Wrexham 1
Replay 2-0

Action Replays

1933 Chester 2 .... Wrexham 0
1934 Bristol C 1 .... Tranmere R 1
Replay 3-0
1935 Tranmere R 1 .... Chester 0
1936 Crewe 2 .... Chester 0
1937 Crewe 1 .... Rhyl 1
Replay 3-1
1938 Shrewsbury 2 .... Swansea 1
1939 S Liverpool 2 ..... Cardiff C 1
1940 Welling T 4 .... Swansea 0
1947 Chester 0 ...... MerthyrTydfil 0
Replay 5-1
1948 Lovells Ath 3 .. Shrewsbury T 0
1949 Merthyr Tydfil 2 .. Swansea T 0
1950 Swansea T 4 .... Wrexham 1
1951 Merthyr Tydfil 1 .... Cardiff C 1
Replay 3-2
1952 Rhyl 4 .... Merthyr Tydfil 3
1953 Rhyl 2 .... Chester 1
1954 Flint Utd 2 .... Chester 0
1955 Barry T 1 .... Chester 1
Replay 4-3
1956 Cardiff C 3 .... Swansea T 2
1957 Wrexham 2 .... Swansea T 2
1958 Wrexham 1 .... Chester 1
Replay 2-0
1959 Cardiff C 2 ..... Lovells Ath 0
1960 Wrexham 0 .... Cardiff C 0
Replay 1-0
1961 Swansea T 3 .... BangorC 1
1962 Bangor C 3 .... Wrexham 1
1963 Borough Utd 2 .. Newport Co1*
1964 Cardiff C 5 .... Bangor C 3*
1965 Cardiff C 8 ...... Wrexham 2*
1966 Swansea T 2 .... Chester 1*
1967 Cardiff C 2 ...... Wrexham 1*
1967 Cardiff C 2 .... Wrexham1*
1968 Cardiff C 6 .... Hereford Utd 1*
1969 Cardiff C 5 ...... Swansea T 1*
1970 Cardiff C 5 .... Chester 0*
1971 Cardiff C 4 .... Wrexham1*
1972 Wrexham 3 ...... Cardiff C 2 *
1973 Cardiff C 5 .... Bangor C 1*
1974 Cardiff C 2 ...... Stourbridge 0*
1975 Wrexham 5 .... Cardiff C 2*

1976 Cardiff C 6 .... Hereford Utd 5*
1977 Shrewsbury T 4 ... Cardiff C 2*
1978 Wrexham 3 .... Bangor C 1*
1979 Shrewsbury T 2 ... Wrexham 1*
1980 Newport Co 5 . Shrewsbury T 1*
1981 Swansea C 2 .. Hereford Utd 1*
1982 Swansea C 2 ...... Cardiff C 1*
1983 Swansea C 4 ,,,,, Wrexham 1*
1984 Shrewsbury T 2 ... Wrexham 0*
1985 Shrewsbury T 5 ... Bangor C 1*
1986 Kidderminster H 1 ... Wrexham1
Replay 2-1
1987 MerthyrTydfil 2 .. Newport Co 2
Replay 1-0
1988 Cardiff C 1 .... Wrexham 0
1989 Swansea C 5 . Kidderminster H 0
1990 Hereford Utd 2 ..... Wrexham 1
1991 Swansea C 2 .... Wrexham 0
1992 Cardiff C 1 ..... Hednesford T 0
1993 Cardiff C 5 .... Rhyl 0
1994 Barry T 2 .... Cardiff C 1
1995 Wrexham 2 .... Cardiff C 1

* Aggregate score

NORTHERN IRELAND

League Champions

1891	Linfield
1892	Linfield
1893	Linfield
1894	Glentoran
1895	Linfield
1896	Distillery
1897	Glentoran
1898	Glenfield
1899	Distillery
1900	Belfast Celtic
1901	Distillery
1902	Linfield
1903	Distillery

THE ANORAK SECTION

1904	Linfield	1960	Glenavon
1905	Glentoran	1961	Linfield
1906	Clifftonville / Distillery	1962	Linfield
1907	Linfield	1963	Distillery
1908	Linfield	1964	Glentoran
1909	Linfield	1965	Derry City
1910	Clifftonville	1966	Linfield
1911	Linfield	1967	Glentoran
1912	Glentoran	1968	Glentoran
1913	Glentoran	1969	Linfield
1914	Linfield	1970	Glentoran
1915	Belfast Celtic	1971	Linfield
1920	Belfast Celtic	1972	Glentoran
1921	Glentoran	1973	Crusaders
1922	Linfield	1974	Coleraine
1923	Linfield	1975	Linfield
1924	Queens Island	1976	Crusaders
1925	Glentoran	1977	Glentoran
1926	Belfast Celtic	1978	Linfield
1927	Belfast Celtic	1979	Linfield
1928	Belfast Celtic	1980	Linfield
1929	Belfast Celtic	1981	Linfield
1930	Linfield	1982	Linfield
1931	Glentoran	1983	Linfield
1932	Linfield	1984	Linfield
1933	Belfast Celtic	1985	Linfield
1934	Linfield	1986	Linfield
1935	Linfield	1987	Linfield
1936	Belfast Celtic	1988	Glentoran
1937	Belfast Celtic	1989	Linfield
1938	Belfast Celtic	1990	Portadown
1939	Belfast Celtic	1991	Portadown
1940	Belfast Celtic	1992	Glentoran
1948	Belfast Celtic	1993	Linfield
1949	Linfield	1994	Linfield
1950	Linfield	1995	Crusadersi
1951	Glentoran		
1952	Glenavon		
1953	Glentoran		
1954	Linfield		
1955	Linfield		
1956	Linfield		
1957	Glentoran		
1958	Ards		
1959	Linfield		

IRISH CUP

1881 Moyola Park 1 . . . .Clifftonville 0
1882 Queen's Islands 2 .Clifftonville 1
1883 Clifftonville 5 . . . . .Ulster 0
1884 Distillery 5 . . . . .Ulster 0

Action Replays

1885 Distillery 2 ....Limavady 0
1886 Distillery 1 ....Limavady 0
Cup and medals withheld "owing to the conduct of both teams".
1887 Ulster 3 ....Clifftonville 1
1888 Clifftonville 2 ......Distillery 1
1889 Distillery 5 ....YMCA 4
1890 Gordon Highlanders 2 ....
.........,Clifftonville 2
Replay 3-0
1891 Linfield 4 ....Ulster 2
1892 Linfield 7 ...The Black Watch 0
1893 Linfield 5 ....Clifftonville 1
1894 Distillery 2 ....Linfield 2
Replay 3-2
1895 Linfield 10 ....Bohemians 1
1896 Distillery 3 ....Glentoran 1
1897 Clifftonville 3 Sherwood Foresters Curragh 1
1898 Linfield 2 ......St Columbs Hall
.... Celtic Derry 0
1899 Linfield 1 ....Glentoran 0
1900 Clifftonville 2 .....Bohemians 1
1901 Clifftonville 1 ....
Freebooters, Dublin 0
1902 Linfield 5 ....Distillery 1
1903 Distillery 3 ....Bohemians 1
1904 Linfield 5 ....Derry Celtic 0
1905 Distillery 3 ....Shelbourne 0
1906 Shelbourne 2 ....Belfast Celtic 0
1907 Clifftonville 0 .....Shelbourne 0
Replay 1-0
1908 Bohemians 1 ......Shelbourne 1
Replay 3-1
1909 Clifftonville 0 .....Bohemians 0
Replay 2-1
1910 Distillery 1 ....Clifftonville 0
1911 Shelbourne 0 ......Bohemians 0
Replay 2-1
1912 Not played: Linfield were awarded the cup
1913 Linfield 2 ....Glentoran 0
1914 Glentoran 3 .... Linfield 1
1915 Linfield 1 ......Belfast Celtic 0
1916 Linfield 1 ....Glentoran 0
1917 Glentoran 2 .....Belfast Celtic 0

1918 Belfast Celtic 0 ....Linfield 0
Replay 0-0
Replay 2-0
1919 Linfield 1 ....Glentoran 1
Replay 0-0
Replay 2-1
1920 Not played: Shelbourne awarded Cup
1921 Glentoran 2 ,, .Glenavon 0
1922 Linfield 2 ....Glenavon 0
1923 Linfield 2 ....Glentoran 0
1924 Queen's Island 1 ...Willowfield 0
1925 Distillery 2 ....Glentoran 1
1926 Belfast Celtic 3 ......Linfield 2
1927 Ards 3 ....Clifftonville 2
1928 Willowfield 1 ....Larne 0
1929 Ballymena Utd 2 Belfast Celtic 1
1930 Linfield 4 .....Ballymena Utd 3
1931 Linfield 3 .....Ballymena Utd 0
1932 Glentoran 2 .... Linfield 1
1933 Glentoran 1 .... Distillery 1
Replay 3-1
1934 Linfield 5 ....Clifftonville 0
1935 Glentoran 0 ....Larne 0
Replay 0-0
Replay 1-0
1936 Linfield 0 ....Derry City 0
Replay 2-1
1937 Belfast Celtic 3 ......Linfield 0
1938 Belfast Celtic 0 ....Bangor 0
Replay 2-0
1939 Linfield 2 .....Ballymena Utd 0
1940 Ballymena Utd 2 ....Glenavon 0
1941 Belfast Celtic 1 ...... Linfield 0
1942 Linfield 3 ....Glentoran 1
1943 Belfast Celtic 1 .....Glentoran 0
1944 Belfast Celtic 3 .... Linfield 1
1945 Linfield 4 ....Glentoran 2
1946 Linfield 3 ....Distillery 0
1947 Belfast Celtic 1 .....Glentoran 0
1948 Linfield 3 ....Coleraine 0
1949 Derry City 3 ....Glentoran 1
1950 Linfield 2 ....Distillery 1
1951 Glentoran 3 ...Ballymena Utd 1
1952 Ards 1 ....Glentoran 0
1953 Linfield 5 ....Coleraine 0

130

THE ANORAK SECTION

1954 Derry City 1 . . . . . . .Glentoran 0
1955 Dundela 3 . . . . .Glenavon 0
1956 Distillery 1 . . . . .Glentoran 0
1957 Glenavon 2 . . . . . .Derry City 0
1950 Ballymena Utd 2 . . . . . .Linfield 0
1959 Glenavon 2 . . . .Ballymena Utd 0
1960 Linfield 5 . . . . .Ards 1
1961 Glenavon 5 . . . . .Linfield 1
1962 Linfield 4 . . . . .Portadown 0
1963 Linfield 2 . . . . .Distillery 1
1964 Derry City 2 . . . . . . .Glentoran 0
1965 Coleraine 2 . . . . .Glenavon 1
1966 Glentoran 2 . . . . .Linfield 0
1967 Crusaders 3 . . . . . . .Glentoran 1
1968 Crusaders 2 . . . . Linfield 0
1969 Ards 4 . . . . .Distillery 2
1970 Linfield 2 . . . . .Ballymena Utd 1
1971 Distillery 3 . . . . .Derry City 0
1972 Coleraine 2 . . . . . . .Portadown 1
1973 Glentoran 3 . . . . .Linfield 2
1974 Ards 2 . . . . .Ballymena Utd 1
1975 Coleraine 1 . . . . .Linfield 1
Replay 0-0
Replay 1-0
1976 Carrick Rangers 2 . . . .Linfield 1
1977 Coleraine 4 . . . . .Linfield 1
1978 Linfield 3 . . . . .Ballymena Utd 1
1979 Clifftonville 3 . . . . .Portadown 2
1980 Linfield 2 . . . . .Crusaders 1
1981 Ballymena Utd 1 . . . .Glenavon 0
1982 Linfield 2 . . . . .Coleraine 1
1983 Glentoran 1 . . . . .Linfield 1
Replay 2-1
1984 Ballymena U 4 Garrick Rangers 1
1985 Glentoran 1 . . . . .Linfield 0
1986 Glentoran 2 . . . . . . .Coleraine 1
1987 Glentoran 1 . . . . Larne 0
1988 Glentoran 1 . . . . .Glenavon 0
1989 Ballymena Utd 1 . . . . . .Larne 0
1990 Glentoran 3 . . . . Porladown 0
1991 Portadown 2 . . . . Glenavon 1
1992 Glenavon 2 . . . . .Linfield 1
1993 Bangor 1 . . . . .Ards 1
Replay 1-1
Replay 1-1
Replay 1-0

1994 Linfield 2 . . . . .Bangor 0
1995 Linfield 3 . . .Carrick Rangers 1

REPUBLIC OF IRELAND

FA LEAGUE CHAMPIONS

Year	Winners	Runners-up
1922	St James's Gate	Bohemians
1923	Shamrock Rovers	Shelbourne
1924	Bohemians	Shelbourne
1925	Shamrock Rovers	Bohemians
1926	Shelbourne	Shamrock Rovers
1927	Shamrock Rovers	Shelbourne
1928	Bohemians	Shelbourne
1929	Shelbourne	Bohemians
1930	Bohemians	Shelbourne
1931	Shelbourne	Dundalk
1932	Shamrock Rovers	Cork
1933	Dundalk	Shamrock Rovers
1934	Bohemians	Cork
1935	Dolphin	St James's Gate
1936	Bohemians	Dolphin
1937	Sligo Rovers	Dundalk
1938	Shamrock Rovers	Waterford
1939	Shamrock Rovers	Sligo Rovers
1940	St James's Gate	Shamrock Rovers
1941	Cork Utd	Waterford
1942	Cork Utd	Shamrock Rovers
1943	Cork Utd	Dundalk
1944	Shelbourne	Limerick
1945	Cork Utd	Limerick
1946	Cork Utd	Drumcondra
1947	Shelbourne	Drumcondra
1948	Drumcondra	Dundalk
1947	Shelbourne	Drumcondra
1948	Drumcondra	Dundalk
1949	Drumcondra	Shelbourne
1950	Cork Ath	Drumcondra
1951	Cork Ath	Shelbourne

131

Action Replays

1952	St Patrick's Ath	Sligo Rovers
1953	Shelbourne	Evergreen Utd
1954	Shamrock Rovers	Drumcondra
1955	St Patrick's Ath	Waterford
1956	St Patrick's Ath	Shamrock R
1957	Shamrock Rovers	Drumcondra
1958	Drumcondra	Shamrock Rovers
1959	Shamrock R	Evergreen Utd
1960	Limerick	Cork Celtic
1961	Drumcondra	St Patrick's Ath
1962	Shelbourne	Cork Celtic
1963	Dundalk	Waterford
1964	Shamrock Rovers	Dundalk
1965	Drumcondra	Shamrock Rovers
1966	Waterford	Shamrock Rovers
1967	Dundalk	Bohemians
1968	Waterford	Dundalk

SAY IT AGAIN
PETER BRACKLEY

"It's a game of two teams."

1969	Waterford	Shamrock Rovers
1970	Waterford	Shamrock Rovers
1971	Cork Hibs	Shamrock Rovers
1972	Waterford	Cork Hibs
1973	Waterford	Finn Harps
1974	Cork Celtic	Bohemians
1975	Bohemians	Athlone T
1976	Dundalk	Finn Harps
1977	Sligo Rovers	Bohemians
1978	Bohemians	Finn Harps
1979	Dundalk	Bohemians
1980	Limerick	Dundalk
1981	Athlone T	Dundalk
1982	Dundalk	Shamrock Rovers
1983	Athlone T	Drogheda Utd
1984	Shamrock Rovers	Bohemians
1985	Shamrock Rovers	Bohemians
1986	Shamrock Rovers	Galway Utd
1987	Shamrock Rovers	Dundalk

1988	Dundalk	St Patrick's Ath
1989	Derry City	Dundalk
1990	St Patrick's Ath	Derry City
1991	Dundalk	Cork City
1992	Shelbourne	Derry City
1993	Cork City	Bohemians
1994	Shamrock Rovers	Cork City
1995	Dundalk	Shelbourne

FAI SENIOR CHALLENGE CUP

1922 St James's Gate 1   Shamrock Rvr 1
   Replay 1-0
1923 Alton Utd 1 ...... Shelbourne 0
1924 Athlone T 1 .... Fordsons 0
1925 Shamrock R 2 .... Shelbourne 1
1926 Fordsons 3 .. Shamrock Rovers 2
1927 Drumcondra 1...... Brideville 0
1928 Bohemians 1 .... Drumcondra 0
1929 Shamrock Rovers 0 Bohemians 0
   Replay 3-0
1930 Shamrock Rovers 1 . Brideville 0
1931 Shamrock Rovers 1 .. Dundalk 0
1932 Shamrock Rovers 1 ... Dolphin 0
1933 Shamrock Rovers 3... Dolphin 3
   Replay 3-0
1934 Cork 2   ..... St James's Gate 1
1935 Bohemians 4 .... Dundalk 3
1936 Shamrock Rovers 2 ..... Cork 1
1937 Waterford 2 ... St James's Gate 1
1938 St James's Gate 2 .... Dundalk 1
1939 Shelbourne 1 .... Sligo Rovers 0
1940 Shamrock R 3 ... Sligo Rovers 0
1941 Cork Utd 2 .... Waterford 2
   Replay 3-1
1942 Dundalk 3 .... Cork Utd   1
1943 Drumcondra 2...... Cork Utd 1
1944 Shamrock Rovers 3 Shelbourne 2
1945 Shamrock Rovers 1. Bohemians 0
1946 Drumcondra 2 ... Shamrock R 1
1947 Cork Utd 2 .... Bohemians 2
   Replay 2-0

132

THE ANORAK SECTION

1948 Shamrock R 2 ... Drumcondra 1
1949 Dundalk 3 .... Shelbourne 0
1950 Transport 2 .... Cork Ath 2
   Replay 2-2
   Replay 3-1
1951 Cork Ath 1 .... Shelbourne 0
1952 Dundalk 1 .... Cork Ath 1
   Replay 3-0
1953 Cork Ath 2 .... Evergreen Utd 2
   Replay 2-1

SAY IT AGAIN
DAVID COLEMAN

"Dont' tell those coming in now the result of that fantastic match. Now let's have another look at Italy's winning goal."

THANK YOU, MR COLEMAN

1954 Drumcondra 1 . St Patrick's Ath0
1955 Shamrock Rovers 1 Drumcondra 0
1956 Shamrock Rovers 3   .Cork Ath 2
1957 Drumcondra 2 ...Shamrock R 0
1958 Dundalk 1 ...Shamrock Rovers 0
1959 St Patrick's Ath 2 ...Waterford 2
   Replay 2-1
1960 Shelbourne 2 ...... Cork Hibs 0
1961 St Patrick's Ath 2 Drumcondra 1
1962 Shamrock Rovers 4 Shelbourne 1
1963 Shelbourne 2 ..... .Cork Hibs 0
1964 Shamrock Rovers 1. Cork Celtic 1
   Replay 2-1
1965 Shamrock Rovers 1 ..Limerick 1
   Replay 1-0
1966 Shamrock Rovers 2 ..Limerick 0
1967 Shamrock R 3 .St Patrick's Ath 2
1968 Shamrock Rovers 3 ..Waterford 0
1969 Shamrock Rovers 1 .Cork Celtic 1
   Replay 4-1

1970 Bohemians 0 .....Sligo Rovers 0
   Replay 0-0
   Replay 2-1
1971 Limerick 0 ....Drogheda 0
   Replay 3-0
1972 Cork Hibs 3 .... Waterford 0
1973 Cork Hibs 0 .....Shelbourne 0
   Replay 1-0
1974 Finn Harps 3...St Patrick's Ath 1
1975 Home Farm 1 ..... Shelbourne 0
1976 Bohemians 1 ...Drogheda Utd 0
1977 Dundalk 2 ....Limerick 0
1978 Shamrock Rovers 1   ...Sligo R 0
1979 Dundalk 2 ....Waterford 0
1980 Waterford 1 ...St Patrick's Ath 0
1981 Dundalk 2 ...... Sligo Rovers -0
1982 Limerick Utd 1 .... Bohemians 0
1983 Sligo Rovers 2 ..... Bohemians 1
1984 University College 2 ..Shamrock Rovers 1
1985 Shamrock R 1 ....Galway Utd 0
1986 Shamrock R 2 ..Waterford Utd 0
1987 Shamrock R 3 ....Dundalk 0
1988 Dundalk 1 .... Derry City 0
1989 Derry City 0 ....Cork City 0
   Replay 1-0
1990 Bray W 3 ....St Francis 0
1991 Galway Utd 1 ....Shamrock R 0
1992 Bohemians 1 ....Cork City 0
1993 Shelbourne 1 .... Dundalk 0
1994 Sligo Rovers 1 .....Derry City 0
1995 Derry City 1 ......Shelbourne 0

ENGLISH FOOTBALLER OF THE YEAR
AWARDED BY THE FOOTBALL WRITERS' ASSOCIATION

1948 Stanley Matthews(Blackpool)
1949 Johnny Carey (Manchester U)
1950 Joe Mercer(Arsenal)
1951 Harry Johnston (Blackpool)
1952 Billy Wright (Wolves)

133

Action Replays

1953 Nat Lofthouse (Bolton Wanderers)
1954 Tom Finney (Preston North End)
1955 Don Revie (Manchester City)
1956 Bert Trautmann (Manchester City)
1957 Tom Finney (Preston North End)
1958 Danny Blanchflower (Tottenham Hotspur)

SAY IT AGAIN
JOHN MOTSON

"The goals made such a difference to the way this game went."

WELL THEY WOULD, WOULDN'T THEY

1959 Syd Owen (Luton Town)
1960 Bill Slater (Wolverhampton Wanderers)
1961 Danny Blanchflower (Tottenham Hotspur)
1962 Jimmy Adamson (Burnley)
1963 Stanley Matthews (Stoke City)
1964 Bobby Moore (West Ham United)
1965 Bobby Collins (Leeds United)
1966 Bobby Charlton (Man Utd)
1967 Jackie Charlton (Leeds United)
1968 George Best (Man. Utd)
1969 Dave Mackay (Derby County) and Tony Book (Manchester City)
1970 Billy Bremner (Leeds United)
1971 Frank McLintock (Arsenal)
1972 Gordon Banks (Stoke City)
1973 Pat Jennings (Tottenham Hotspur)
1974 Ian Callaghan (Liverpool)
1975 Alan Mullery (Fulham)
1976 Kevin Keegan (Liverpool)
1977 Emlyn Hughes (Liverpool)
1978 Kenny Burns (Nottingham Forest)
1979 Kenny Dalglish (Liverpool)
1980 Terry McDermott (Liverpool)
1981 Frans Thijssen (Ipswich Town)
1982 Steve Perryman (Tottenham Hotspur)
1983 Kenny Dalglish (Liverpool)
1984 Ian Rush (Liverpool)
1985 Neville Southall (Everton)
1986 Gary Lineker (Everton)
1987 Clive Allen (Tottenham Hotspur)
1988 John Barnes (Liverpool)
1989 Steve Nicol (Liverpool)
1990 John Barnes (Liverpool)
1991 Gordon Strachan (Leeds United)
1992 Gary Lineker (Tottenham Hotspur)
1993 Chris Waddle (Sheffield Wednesday)
1994 Alan Shearer (Blackburn Rovers)
1995 Jorgen Klinsmann (Tottenham Hotspur)
1996 Eric Cantona (Man. Utd)

SCOTTISH FOOTBALLER OF THE YEAR

1965 Billy McNeill (Celtic)
1966 John Greig (Rangers)
1967 Ronnie Simpson (Celtic)
1968 Gordon Wallace (Raith Rovers)
1969 Bobby Murdoch (Celtic)
1970 Pat Stanton (Hibernian)
1971 Martin Bochan (Aberdeen)
1972 Dave Smith (Rangers)
1973 George Connelly (Celtic)
1974 Scotland World Cup squad
1975 Sandy Jardine (Rangers)
1976 John Greig (Rangers)
1977 Danny McGrain (Celtic)
1978 Derek Johnstone (Rangers)

THE ANORAK SECTION

1979 Andy Ritchie (Morton)
1980 Gordon Strachan (Aberdeen)
1981 Alan Rough (Partick Thistle)
1982 Paul Sturrock (Dundee United)
1983 Charlie Nicholas (Celtic)
1984 Willie Miller (Aberdeen)
1985 Hamish McAlpine (Dundee United)
1986 Sandy Jardine (Hearts)
1987 Brian McClair (Celtic)
1988 Paul McStay (Celtic)
1989 Richard Gough (Rangers)
1990 Alex McLeish (Aberdeen)
1991 Maurice Malpas (Dundee United)
1992 Ally McCoist (Rangers)
1993 Andy Goram (Rangers)
1994 Mark Hateley (Rangers)
1995 Brian Laudrup (Rangers)
1996 Paul Gascoigne (Rangers)

FIFA WORLD FOOTBALLER OF THE YEAR

1991 Lothar Matthaus (Germany)
1992 Marco Van Basten (Holland)
1993 Roberto Baggio (Italy)
1994 Romario (Brazil)

WORLD FOOTBALLER OF THE YEAR
AWARDED BY WORLD SOCCER MAGAZINE

1982 Paulo Rossi (Juventus & Italy)
1983 Zico (Udinese & Brazil)
1984 Michel Platini (Juventus & France)
1985 Michel Platini (Juventus & France)
1986 Diego Maradona (Napoli & Argentina)
1987 Ruud Gullit (AC Milan & Holland)
1988 Marco Van Basten (Milan & Holland)
1989 Ruud Gullit (Milan & Holland)
1990 Lothar Matthaus (Internatzionale & W. Germany)
1991 Jean-Pierre Papin (Marseille & France)
1992 Marco Van Basten (Milan & Holland)
1993 Roberto Baggio (Juventus & Italy)
1994 Paolo Maldini (Milan & Italy)

AFRICAN FOOTBALLER OF THE YEAR
AWARDED BY FRANCE FOOTBALL MAGAZINE

1970 Salif Keita (Mali)
1971 Ibrahim Sunday (Ghana)
1972 Cherif Souleymane (Guinea)
1973 Tshimen Bwanga (Zaire)
1974 Paul Moukila (Congo)
1975 Ahmed Faras (Morocco)
1976 Roger Milla (Cameroon)
1977 Tarak Dhiab (Tunisia)
1978 Karim Abdoul Razak (Ghana)
1979 Thomas N'Kono (Cameroon)
1980 Manga Onguene (Cameroon)
1981 Lakhdar Belloumi (Algeria)
1982 Thomas N'Kono (Cameroon)
1983 Mahmoud Al Khatib (Egypt)
1984 Theophile Abega (Cameroon)
1985 Mohamed Timoumi (Morocco)
1986 Badou Zaki (Morocco)
1987 Rabah Madjer (Algeria)
1988 Kalusha Bwalya (Zambia)
1989 George Weah (Liberia)
1990 Roger Milla (Cameroon)
1991 Abedi Pele (Ghana)
1992 Abedi Pele (Ghana)
1993 Abedi Pele (Ghana)
1994 George Weah (Liberia)

African Confederation Player of the Year Award

1993 Rashidi Yekini (Nigeria)
1994 Emanuel Amunike (Nigeria)

SAY IT AGAIN

GLENN HODDLE

"Football's all about 90 minutes..."

GLENN HODDLE

"Football's about 90 minutes on the day; it's about tomorrows really."

THIS MAN IS THE ENGLAND MANAGER!

EUROPEAN FOOTBALLER OF THE YEAR
AWARDED BY FRANCE FOOTBALL MAGAZINE

1956 Stanley Matthews (Blackpool)
1957 Alfredo Di Stefano (Real Madrid)
1958 Raymond Kopa (Real Madrid)
1959 Alfredo Di Stefano (Real Madrid)
1960 Luis Suarez (Barcelona)
1961 Omar Sivori (Juventus)
1962 Josef Masopust (Dukla Prague)
1963 Lev Yashin (Moscow Dynamo)
1964 Denis Law (Man. Utd)
1965 Eusebio (Benfica)
1966 Bobby Charlton (Man Utd)
1967 Florian Albert (Ferencvaros)
1968 George Best (Man. Utd)
1969 Gianni Rivera (Milan)
1970 Gerd Muller (Bayern Munich)
1971 Johan Cruyff (Ajax)
1972 Franz Beckenbauer (Bayern Munich)
1973 Johan Cruyff (Barcelona)
1974 Johan Cruyff (Barcelona)
1975 Oleg Blokhin (Dynamo Kiev)
1976 Franz Beckenbauer (Bayern Munich)
1977 Allan Simonsen (Borussia MG)
1978 Kevin Keegan (Hamburg)
1979 Kevin Keegan (Hamburg)
1980 Karl-Heinz Rumenigge (Bayern Munich)
1981 Karl-Heinz Rumenigge (Bayern Munich)
1982 Paolo Rossi (Juventus)
1983 Michel Platini (Juventus)
1984 Michel Platini (Juventus)
1985 Michel Platini (Juventus)
1986 Igor Belanov (Dynamo Kiev)
1987 Ruud Gullit (Milan)
1988 Marco Van Basten (Milan)
1989 Marco Van Basten (Milan)
1990 Lothar Matthaus (Inter)
1991 Jean-Pierre Papin (Marseille)
1992 Marco Van Basten (Milan)
1993 Roberto Baggio (Juventus)
1994 Hristo Stoichkov (Barcelona)

SOUTH AMERICAN FOOTBALLER OF THE YEAR

1971 Tostao (Brazil)
1972 Teofilio Cubillas (Peru)
1973 Pele (Brazil)
1974 Elias Figueroa (Chile)
1975 Elias Figueroa (Chile)

1976 Elias Figueroa (Chile)
1977 Zico (Brazil)
1978 Mario Kempes (Argentina)
1979 Diego Maradona (Argentina)
1980 Diego Maradona (Argentina)
1981 Zico (Brazil)
1982 Zico (Brazil)
1983 Socrates (Brazil)
1984 Enzo Francescoli (Uruguay)
1985 Romero (Brazil)
1986 Alzamendi (Uruguay)
1987 Carlos Valderrama (Colombia)
1988 Ruben Paz (Uruaguay)
1989 Bebeto (Brazil)
1990 Raul Amarilla (Paraguay)
1991 Oscar Ruggeri (Argentina)
1992 Rai (Brazil)
1993 Carlos Valderrama (Colombia)
1994 Cafu (Brazil)

ASIAN FOOTBALLER OF THE YEAR

1990 Kim Joo-sung (S. Korea)
1991 Kim Joo-sung (S. Korea)
1992 not awarded
1993 Kaziu Miura (Japan)
1994 said Al-Owiran (S. Arabia)

OCEANIA FOOTBALLER OF THE YEAR

1990 Robby Slater (Australia)
1991 Wynton Rufer (N. Zealand)
1992 Wynton Rufer (N. Zealand)
1993 Robby Slater (Australia)
1994 Aurelio Vidmar (Australian)

SAY IT AGAIN

RON WYLIE

"I don't really believe in targets, because my next target is to beat Stoke City."

SO IT'S A GOOD JOB YOU DON'T HAVE ANY TARGETS THEN!

Action Replays

EUROPEAN GOLDEN BOOT

Awarded to the leading goalscorer in Europe.
The competition was ended in 1991.

Year	Player	Club	Goals
1968	Eusebio	Benfica	42
1969	Petar Jekov	CSKA Sofia	36
1970	Gerd Muller	Bayern Munich	38
1971	Josip Skoblar	Olympique Marseille	44
1972	Gerd Muller	Bayern Munich	40
1973	Eusebio	Benfica	40
1974	Hector Yazalde	Sporting Lisbon	46
1975	Dudu Georgescu	Dinamo Bucharest	33
1976	Sotiris Kaiafas	Omonia Nicosia	39
1977	Oudu Georgescu	Dinamo Bucharest	47
1978	Hans Krank	Rapid Vienna	41
1979	Kees Kist	AZ Alkmaar	34
1980	Erwin Vandenburgh	Lierse	39
1981	Georgi Slavkov	Trakia Plovdiv	31
1982	Wim Kieft	Ajax	32
1983	Fernando Gomes	Porto	36
1984	Ian Rush	Liverpool	32
1985	Fernando Gomes	Porto	39
1986	Marco Van Basten	Ajax	37
1987	Rodion Camataru	Dinamo Bucharest	44
1988	Tanju Colak	Galatasaray	39
1989	Dorin Mateut	Dinamo Bucharest	43
1990	Hugo Sanchez	Real Madrid	38
	Hristo Stoichkov	CSKA Sofia	38
1991	Darko Pancev	Red Star Belgrade	34

ENGLAND WOMEN'S CHALLENGE CUP

1971	Southampton 4	Stewarton & Thistle 1
1972	Southampton 3	Lee's Ladies 2
1973	Southampton 2	Westhorn Utd 0
1974	Foxdens 2	Southampton 1
1975	Southampton 4	Warminster 2

THE ANORAK SECTION

1976	Southampton 2	QPR 1
1977	QPR 1	Southampton 0
1978	Southampton 8	QPR 2
1979	Southampton 1	Lowestoft 0
1980	St Helens 1	Preston North End 0
1981	Southampton 4	St Helens 2
1982	Lowestoft 2	Cleveland Spartans 0
1983	Doncaster Belles 3	St Helens 2
1984	Howbury Grange 4	Doncaster Belles 2
1985	Friends of Fulham 2	Doncaster Belles 0
1986	Norwich 4	Doncaster Belles 3
1987	Doncaster Belles 2	St Helens 0
1988	Doncaster Belles 3	Leasowe Pacific 1
1989	Leasowe Pacific 3	Friends of Fulham 2
1990	Doncaster Belles 1	Friends of Fulham 0
1991	Millwall Lionesses 1	Doncaster Belles 0
1992	Doncaster Belles 4	Red Star Southampton 0
1993	Arsenal 3	Doncaster Belles 0
1994	Doncaster Belles 1	Knowsley Utd 0
1995	Arsenal 3	Liverpool 2
1996	Croydon 1	Liverpool 1

Croydon won 4-3 on penalties

Women's Football Association National League

1991-1992...... Doncaster Belles
1992-1993...... Arsenal Ladies
1993-1994...... Doncaster Belles

Football Association Women's Premier League

1994-1995...... Arsenal Ladies
1995-1996...... Croydon WFC

Women's World Cup

1991 USA 2...... Norway 1
1995 Norway 2... Germany 0